CYBERSECURITY AND PRIVACY LAW

IN A NUTSHELL®

JAY P. KESAN
University of Illinois at Urbana-Champaign

CAROL M. HAYES
University of Illinois at Urbana-Champaign

WEST
ACADEMIC
PUBLISHING

Nutshell Series, In a Nutshell and the Nutshell Logo are trademarks registered in the U.S. Patent and Trademark Office.

© 2019 LEG, Inc. d/b/a West Academic
    444 Cedar Street, Suite 700
    St. Paul, MN 55101
    1-877-888-1330

West, West Academic Publishing, and West Academic are trademarks of West Publishing Corporation, used under license.

Printed in the United States of America

ISBN: 978-1-63460-272-3

For Rosalyn
—J.P.K.

ACKNOWLEDGMENTS

The content of this nutshell is based in part on the authors' research over the last decade. We express our gratitude to the National Research Council for their feedback concerning our active defense research. We also appreciate all of our opportunities for collaboration within the Critical Infrastructure Resilience Institute, a Center of Excellence of the Department of Homeland Security. We would also like to thank Katie Bethke and Kyle Dettro for their excellent research assistance.

Some of the content contained in this volume is adapted from works that the authors published in the Harvard Journal of Law and Technology, the Washington and Lee Law Review, the Indiana Law Journal, the Michigan State Law Review, the Arizona Law Review, the Minnesota Law Review, the Illinois Law Review, the Encyclopedia of Cloud Computing, and the International Encyclopedia of Digital Communication and Society. We are also thankful to the editors of these publications.

OUTLINE

TABLE OF CASES

References are to Pages

CYBERSECURITY AND PRIVACY LAW

IN A NUTSHELL®

CHAPTER 1
INTRODUCTION

Cybersecurity is a serious concern in the modern age. Our real lives and digital lives are often inextricably linked. Attorneys and their clients are significantly affected by the implications of cybersecurity events. Data security is also becoming an ethical issue for attorneys. To protect client information, attorneys increasingly have to take active steps to protect data, not just refrain from making disclosures.

Cybersecurity policy issues implicate both private and public international law in addition to domestic law. The cybersecurity climate has created an environment where general practitioners should be aware of the international implications of certain actions. The overlap of civilian and military information infrastructure means that civilians could be directly affected by cyberwar between sovereign nations. In this nutshell, we will provide an overview of many of the major legal issues relating to cybersecurity. We decided to briefly introduce major international cybersecurity issues first in this chapter in part because there is no easy line between domestic and international in cybersecurity. The Internet provides a forum that is at once the world's largest conference room and the world's largest battlefield.

Cybersecurity is not an area where attorneys can afford to remain uninformed. It affects governments, the military, big businesses, small businesses, and the law firms themselves. Regardless of an attorney's clients or practice areas, as long as the Internet still exists and people still use computers throughout their personal and professional lives, data security will be an underlying concern in virtually everything that the attorney does.

I. INTERNATIONAL CYBERSECURITY

International cybersecurity issues have largely emerged over the last decade. In 2007, unidentified attackers hit Estonian government systems with politically-motivated cyberattacks. In 2008, cyberattacks against Georgia coincided with the beginning of that country's war with Russia. In 2010, discussions of cyberwar exploded when researchers discovered Stuxnet, a pernicious and resilient worm that exploited four zero-day vulnerabilities in order to sabotage nuclear centrifuges in Iran. Zero days are security flaws that are unknown to the publisher before they are exploited, and they are generally thought to be fairly rare, which is why it is impressive that Stuxnet exploited four of them. Stuxnet forced the control systems of the centrifuges to spin the centrifuges faster than they were supposed to go, causing them to burn out, while preserving the appearance of proper functioning from the perspective of the person watching the controls.[1] The broken centrifuges are thought to have slowed

---

[1]   Roland L. Trope & Stephen J. Humes, *Before Rolling Blackouts Begin: Briefing Boards on Cyber Attacks That Target and Degrade the Grid*, 40 WM. MITCHELL L. REV. 647, 675 (2014).

down the uranium enrichment process in the affected facilities.

Stuxnet may be the first well-known demonstration of the ability to use cyberattacks to harm physical infrastructure, but it was neither the first nor the last. In 2007, researchers conducted a test at Idaho National Laboratories, commonly called the "Aurora Generator Test."[2] The Aurora Generator Test revealed that it was possible for a hacker to use malicious commands to cause a power generator turbine to overheat and damage the equipment, showing the very real potential for a cyberattack to act like a physical attack. In December 2014, a report from Germany indicated that a cyberattack had caused significant damage to a German steel mill. Cyberattacks have so far disrupted Ukraine's power grid on at least two high profile occasions, once in December 2015 and again in December 2016.

II. DOMESTIC CYBERSECURITY

Cyberattacks have had significant impacts on domestic issues as well. The number of major hacking events that occurred in 2011 alone set the stage for making cybersecurity a vital concern in United States policy. Prominent targets that year included government contractors, security technology firms, and entertainment companies like Sony Computer Entertainment. Activism using cyberattack methods, also called hacktivism, gained global attention with

---

[2]   Clay Wilson, Cong. Research Serv., RL32114, Botnets, Cybercrime, and Cyberterrorism: Vulnerabilities and Policy Issues for Congress 20 (2008).

events like Operation Arab Spring, where political activists were supported by the loose-knit hacker collective, Anonymous.

One of the high profile American targets in 2011 was the government cybersecurity contractor HBGary Federal. When company leaders announced that they were preparing to unmask Anonymous, the hacker collective responded by breaking into HBGary Federal's systems and downloading sensitive information from company email accounts. HBGary's ill-fated attempt to take on Anonymous drew criticism from some, with Brown and Metcalf observing that "[u]nfortunately, [the CEO] failed to follow a basic rule—before taking on a hacker group, ensure your computer systems are secure."[3]

High profile attacks have persisted, and a lot of security breaches have impacted innocent individuals whose personal information is stolen. In 2013, Target suffered a major security breach during the holiday shopping season when hackers stole millions of payment records. The breach at Target may have affected as much as a third of the United States population. In November 2014, hackers released mountains of sensitive information from servers at Sony Pictures Entertainment, threatening further harm if Sony Pictures went forward with its planned release of The Interview, a comedy about journalists going to North Korea. In March 2015, Premera Blue Cross announced that it had been

---

[3] Gary D. Brown & Andrew O. Metcalf, *Easier Said Than Done: Legal Reviews of Cyber Weapons*, 7 J. NAT'L SECURITY L. & POL'Y 115, 126 (2014).

hacked, resulting in the leak of the health records of eleven million people. Later in 2015, the federal Office of Personnel Management (OPM) announced their discovery of a massive theft of the personal information of government employees and applicants for security clearances. While only a few million were initially thought to be affected by the OPM hack, that number soon leapt to 21.5 million. The 2017 breach of Equifax may have exposed the complete credit history of over 145 million American adults.

Security breaches like these are a major area of concern, and the threat of more such breaches is continually growing. However, detection of these breaches is not always easy, and sometimes someone other than the victim discovers it first. Verizon's 2017 Data Beach Investigations Report found that 27% of data breaches were discovered by a third party.

When a company experiences an information security breach, these breaches can harm systems, degrade business operations, and damage consumer confidence. A 2015 study by the Ponemon Institute estimated that when confidential information is stolen, the cost of addressing the breach averages $217 per record in the United States.[4] By 2018, that had increased to $258 per record breached.[5] After the Target breach, the cost to banks was reported to be approximately $240 million just for replacing affected cards, not including any fraudulent charges that followed the breach. The risks are compounded

---

[4]   Ponemon Institute, 2015 Cost of Data Breach Study.

[5]   Ponemon Institute, 2018 Cost of Data Breach Study.

if the company fails to take basic precautions, like maintaining firewalls, keeping anti-virus software up to date, and encrypting sensitive information like passwords and credit card numbers.

Security breaches can open companies up to all kinds of liability, including sanctions from the Federal Trade Commission (FTC). In 2015, the Third Circuit held that the FTC can sue companies that use inadequate security practices under its Section 5 authority to prevent unfair or deceptive acts or practices.[6] However, the FTC tends to rely on ad hoc adjudication, and the penalties authorized under Section 5 may be inadequate to deter bad security behavior. The Third Circuit decision concerned the FTC's litigation against the Wyndham hotel group, which was first filed in 2012 after the discovery of multiple data breaches. This litigation went on for several years before the parties settled. Wyndham stored customer credit cards in an unencrypted format, did not use firewalls, and individual hotels were often connected to Wyndham's central network with easily discoverable default usernames and passwords. The final settlement with the FTC only addressed future monitoring and did not include any financial penalties.[7] This is largely typical of FTC adjudications, where settlements and consent orders often require ongoing monitoring without imposing financial liability for the first adjudication.

---

[6]   F.T.C. v. Wyndham Worldwide Corp., 799 F.3d 236 (3d Cir. 2015).

[7]   Stipulated Order for Injunction, F.T.C. v. Wyndham Worldwide Corp., Dec. 11, 2015.

There is a broad range of potential consequences for a cybersecurity incident. The danger that a thief could make purchases with a stolen credit card is very real, but the threat also goes beyond dollars and cents. Virtually every industry is reliant on effective cybersecurity. Ransomware attacks on hospitals can even put patients' lives in jeopardy by blocking medical professionals from obtaining accurate and up to date patient information. In the legal field, safeguarding client information has become an ethical matter, not just a technological or financial matter.

This text is not intended to be alarmist. Instead, our goal is to empower attorneys to learn about these risks and incorporate knowledge about these risks in their professional and personal lives. There are risks associated with relying on digital information storage, but there are risks associated with almost everything. The trick is to be aware of the risks and take steps to mitigate them. Risks associated with driving can be mitigated by wearing seatbelts, having routine maintenance done on vehicles, and adhering to traffic laws. Information security risks are similar, but the threat is not as widely understood, so risk mitigation can be a challenge. With time, however, information security practices will become second nature, like buckling a seatbelt.

In the meantime, uncertainty permeates the legal profession when addressing issues of privacy and security. In this text, we will explore case law, legislation, and administrative actions that attorneys should keep in mind, whether they are

working on a case about cybersecurity or just want to
know more about security and privacy in the age of
the Internet.

CHAPTER 2

CYBERSECURITY TECHNOLOGY AND ACTORS

This chapter will provide an introduction to technology relevant to cybersecurity. While being technologically savvy is increasingly common among lawyers, most lawyers do not have a technical background. Some lawyers can build and fix their own computers, but such expertise is not necessary to understand and appreciate legal issues relating to cybersecurity. However, some knowledge of concepts and terminology is important, which is why we have prepared this chapter as a technology primer for lawyers.

I. SECURITY STORYTIME

Because lawyers are accustomed to detailed hypotheticals, we decided to introduce common elements of cybersecurity events in that familiar format. What follows is a story that will provide characters and examples to which we will refer throughout this chapter. Any resemblance to real individuals or companies is completely coincidental.

Carrie is the CEO of Compbiz, an industry leader in software solutions. Carrie and her employees are careful, but as with any software, bugs occasionally make it into the finished product.

Sam is the CEO of a computer security company. His company, Securesoft, has become an industry leader in security solutions. Securesoft's business activities run the spectrum of security. Securesoft has divisions that specialize in finding software vulnerabilities, preventing the spread of computer viruses, developing new encryption technologies, and detecting intrusions.

Robert is the CEO of Retailco, an online retailer. Retailco uses products by both Compbiz and Securesoft.

Because a cybersecurity story wouldn't be complete without a hacker, we have three: Wilma, George, and Brian. Wilma works for Securesoft and solves cybersecurity problems as part of her job. George is a systems administrator who does freelance security work and sometimes sells information to companies about vulnerabilities in their products, often in the form of a "bug bounty." Brian is a coder who supplements his income by hacking into other systems, stealing information, and selling that information on the black market. These three represent, respectively, the white hat, grey hat, and black hat hacker categories often referenced in cybersecurity commentary.

In the most recent release, Compbiz's flagship product adds a new feature that allows users to have more control over databases when editing them remotely. This is a major plus for Retailco, because it makes it easier for problems to be fixed quickly instead of waiting for a coder to get to the office. Unfortunately, one of the lines of code has a flaw that could allow unauthorized users to seize control of the database.

George and Brian find the flaw around the same time. George contacts Compbiz to tell them about the flaw and says that he would like to demonstrate it at a security conference in a few months, giving Compbiz plenty of time to patch the flaw. Brian, meanwhile, builds malware that takes advantage of the flaw and starts trying to figure out how to use it to steal things like credit card numbers from company databases. By the time Brian's exploit is ready, Compbiz has patched the flaw for users of version 2.1 of the software. Unfortunately, Retailco has not updated their systems and thus is still using version 2.0.

Brian deploys a website that includes malicious code taking advantage of the security flaw. Thanks to an earlier virus that he used, he had already compromised thousands of computers and turned them into botnets to carry out his orders on a large scale. He uses one of his botnets to disseminate phishing emails to a large list of email addresses, including hundreds of Retailco.com addresses. The email purports to be about tax return information, but clicking on the link in the email will take the user to Brian's malicious website. Andrew, an executive assistant at Retailco, receives the phishing email and clicks on the link. Because Andrew is using version 2.0 of Compbiz's product, his computer becomes infected. Brian notices this while looking through the results of his phishing campaign, and uses Andrew's infected machine to access Retailco's customer database. Brian manages to download 3,000 customer profiles, including unencrypted credit card information, before triggering Retailco's Securesoft brand intrusion detection alarm.

Brian promptly absconds with the information, leaving Retailco to deal with the fallout. He sells the list of credit card numbers on the black market. Most of the stolen credit cards were issued by BigBank, which provides fraud protection for customers. Most of the cards were canceled before they could be used, but BigBank still has to pay $100,000 in fraudulent charges and an additional $10,000 to reissue all of the affected cards.

As an attorney, any of these actors might end up as your client. As CEOs, Carrie, Sam, and Robert are all likely to be called upon to explain or defend their companies' actions. Retailco might be sued by BigBank or its customers. Compbiz might need advice about possible legal liability for their product. Compbiz also might seek an injunction against George to keep him from presenting his research findings, or they might allege that Securesoft did not perform as promised in its investigation after the breach. Retailco's customers might subscribe to a credit monitoring service if their information was compromised.

The above example is one of the more straightforward examples. Hackers can target less protected subcontractors to get access to a larger organization. This is what happened with Target, where the hackers' path into Target's system was through a third party refrigeration contractor. There are also significant risks that hackers could compromise critical infrastructure like bulk power systems, or even target airplanes, cars, and medical devices.

II. COMPUTERS AND SOFTWARE

"If you wish to make an apple pie from scratch, you must first invent the universe," Carl Sagan once sagely observed. Many interpret this statement as referring to the way that everything is built using earlier innovations. Nothing exists in a vacuum. The more appreciation a baker has for the science of cooking, the better able the baker is to tweak the recipe for the best outcome. This chapter is about that kind of appreciation within the cybersecurity context. Anyone can follow a recipe. Improvements require a decent understanding of what makes the recipe work.

Modern innovations in computing and communications technologies started to take shape in the middle of the twentieth century. Many important elements relating to computers and security were developed during World War II. For example, Allied forces recruited the mathematicians who broke the Enigma code that the German military used to encrypt messages, contributing to advances in cryptography. Afterwards, computer technology innovations started to focus on private sector uses in addition to military uses. Early computers could take up entire rooms. Intel made the first microprocessor commercially available in 1971, and as computers started to shrink, the personal computing market grew.

Meanwhile, researchers were developing the Internet, with one of the first major demonstrations of its capabilities taking place in 1977. Before Internet research began, computers were not designed to interface with other computers. To enable a worldwide network of computers, the first Internet researchers had to standardize the technologies involved. One way that they did this was through the creation of protocols like IP and TCP that allowed computers to talk with each other. IP stands for Internet Protocol, and TCP stands for Transmission Control Protocol. IP is focused on getting packets of data from point A to point B, and TCP protects the integrity of the packets of data so that the packets arrive at point B in the same shape that they were in when they left point A.[1]

Computers accomplish tasks based on input from the operator. To simplify this for users, computer programmers write instructions for the computer that users can utilize for their specific tasks. The instructions ultimately must be in machine language, which consists entirely of numbers and would be unreadable for most humans. Higher level programming languages, like C#, allow programmers to write the instructions in something that resembles human language, and the instructions are then compiled into machine language and executed by the computer. This package of instructions is commonly called software.

---

[1]   J.R. Okin, THE INTERNET REVOLUTION: THE NOT-FOR-DUMMIES GUIDE TO THE HISTORY, TECHNOLOGY, AND USE OF THE INTERNET 159–60 (2005).

As modern life places more and more demands on software functionality, software becomes more complicated. Some Internet policy commentators have suggested addressing information security problems by giving software programmers incentives to release more secure code. However, no incentive could completely remove software vulnerabilities. Security holes are not an indication of bad coders. Complex software packages simply have to contain a lot of instructions for computers, creating too many opportunities for error. Before criticizing coders for software flaws, attorneys would do well to remember how taxing it can be to pore through a 10,000 word brief or contract looking for any typographical errors. A relatively simple mobile application may contain 10,000 lines of code, while the 2011 version of the Android operating system had over a million lines of code. Software gets more complicated the more it does. It takes fifty million lines of code to run the Large Hadron Collider at CERN, and Facebook relies on over sixty million lines of code. Imagine checking that for typos.

And software is everywhere, including your car. Modern high-end cars may rely on software that contains a hundred million lines of code. This volume of code can make it possible to hide functionalities that flout regulations. Volkswagen skidded into a scandal in September 2015 when it was revealed that millions of their diesel vehicles contained software designed to produce false emission test results.

Bugs in software are the foundation of most cybersecurity threats. Software flaws are an underlying factor in many breaches because such flaws often make external intrusions possible. But as seen in our example story, many if not most of these breaches are probably actually a combination of software flaws and human error. "Black hat" hacker Brian's exploit would not have accomplished much if it had not been for Andrew, the careless Retailco employee who clicked on a link in a phishing email. Some of the responsibility also falls on the systems administrator at Retailco who failed to update systems with the new version of Compbiz's product. Compbiz might also be at fault for releasing the flawed software to begin with, but their liability is likely limited. Contractual terms in end user licensing agreements (EULAs) often protect software manufacturers from liability for security flaws.

Researchers at Carnegie Mellon University estimate that the average software developed in the United States has 6,000 software flaws per million lines of code, and between one and five percent of software flaws are security vulnerabilities. Even exceptional software could be expected to have several hundred flaws per million lines of code.[2] If even ten percent of security vulnerabilities have critical security implications, a software package like Windows 7 with 40 million lines of code could still have dozens of critical security holes and hundreds of non-critical security flaws. With popular consumer

---

[2]   Carol Woody & Nancy Mead, *Using Quality Metrics and Security Methods to Predict Software Assurance*, SEI BLOG (June 20, 2016), https://insights.sei.cmu.edu/sei_blog/2016/06/using-quality-metrics-and-security-methods-to-predict-software-assurance.html.

products relying on tens of millions of lines of code, the danger of security flaws is omnipresent. In our example, Andrew probably should have known better than to click on a link in a questionable email, but that bell cannot be unrung. All Retailco can do now is try to manage the damage.

III. HACKING

There are a lot of buzzwords about cybersecurity and technology that some readers may not be familiar with. In this section, we provide some background about these terms and the underlying hacking-related activities.

The first buzzword that we should explain is "hacking." In basic terms, hacking includes using tools in a way that is designed to let the actor do something other than what the tools are intended for. At its most benign, hacking is an exercise in ingenuity that can result in new and better outcomes, as the many "life hack" videos and posts online demonstrate. But since we are concerned with the cybersecurity context, benign hacking will be less prevalent in our discussion.

"Social engineering" is a term that has been applied to deceptive behaviors in certain contexts. In information security, social engineering is often an early stage of hacking where the attacker convinces a gatekeeper to provide the attacker with access. But social engineering can also be the whole scam. For example, there exist black market services that promise clients refunds on expensive online purchases. The plan is often for the hired individual to convince customer service representatives that the item was not received. The clients pay the person either a flat fee or a percentage of the purchase price, and if successful, the original purchase price is refunded and the client has an expensive product at a deep discount. Refunding services like this are available on black market forums online. Many of these forums are located in unindexed areas of the web. These areas are broadly referred to as the "deep web," and the websites that spring up to offer illegal services are often viewed as part of the "darknet."

Zero-day vulnerabilities and exploits, often simply called "zero days," are a highly valuable type of software vulnerability. Zero-day vulnerabilities were unknown to the maker of the software before the vulnerability was used destructively. When such a vulnerability has been weaponized, it may be referred to as a zero-day exploit. The first major cyberweapon, Stuxnet, used four zero day exploits. Zero days are frequently bought and sold in markets of varying legality.

Computer hacking proceeds in a predictable pattern. System vulnerabilities are identified, analyzed, and exploited. In our example story, George and Brian were both freelance hackers who identified the same vulnerability. Brian, however, comes from the "black hat" camp and wanted to use the information for his own benefit, while George fell more into the white or grey camp and acted with the ultimate goal of bringing about security improvements. Because the vulnerability that Brian exploited was known and patched prior to its use, it should not be referred to as a zero-day vulnerability. Still, media coverage often overuses the term, much to the chagrin of many security professionals, who also often cringe at the use of "cyber" as a noun.

Knowledge of vulnerabilities can be used to repair systems as easily as it can be used to exploit them. This dual-use nature of vulnerability knowledge creates a significant cybersecurity policy problem. Assuming that security exploitations are a societal ill, it is in the interests of society to encourage good faith research to discover and fix software vulnerabilities. How should policy encourage George while discouraging Brian? One danger of punitive cybercrime laws is that such laws may be more effective at deterring benign hacking than they are at deterring malicious hacking. Compared to hackers who intentionally seek to undermine the law, hackers with good intentions are much more likely to be deterred by laws that make their actions illegal.

a.   CYBERATTACKS

In the modern lexicon, all types of computer intrusions are regularly called "cyberattacks," but many professionals and commentators in the field would assert that indiscriminate use of the term "cyberattack" is incorrect. The National Research Council's 2009 report about cyberattack capabilities ("the NRC report") defines cyberattack as "the use of deliberate actions—perhaps over an extended period of time—to alter, disrupt, deceive, degrade, or destroy adversary computer systems or networks or the information and/or programs resident in or transiting these systems or networks."[3] Cyberattacks can also be viewed as actions that target the integrity, authenticity, and availability of components or devices on a network.[4] Organizational information security practices often emphasize the similar CIA Triad: Confidentiality, Integrity, and Availability.

The 2009 NRC report distinguishes between cyberattacks, which are destructive in nature, and cyber exploitations, which are non-destructive actions to extract confidential information. However, it can be hard to distinguish between cyberattacks and cyber exploitations, because both use similar technology, with the primary difference being the goals of the two. A cyber attacker's goal may be to destroy information, for example, while the exploiter's goal is just to copy the information or observe network activity. Duqu, a cyber exploit with some similarities to Stuxnet, demonstrates the overlap between the two concepts. Researchers at Symantec posit that Duqu's purpose was to collect information for future attacks.[5] In the alternative, cyberattacks and cyber exploitations can both be referred to as cyber intrusions. We will primarily

---

[3]   NAT'L RESEARCH COUNCIL OF THE NAT'L ACADS., TECHNOLOGY, POLICY, LAW, AND ETHICS REGARDING U.S. ACQUISITION AND USE OF CYBERATTACK CAPABILITIES, 10–11 (William A. Owens et al. eds., 2009).

[4]   Herbert S. Lin, *Offensive Cyber Operations and the Use of Force*, 4 J. NAT'L SECURITY L. & POL'Y 63, 67 (2010).

[5]   Posting of Symantec Security Response to Symantec Official Blog, Oct. 24, 2011.

refer to cybersecurity events generally as cyberattacks or cyber incidents.

Another common term in cybersecurity is "advanced persistent threat." APTs are typically directed at specific targets. APTs generally involve malware and external command and control capabilities to allow the outsider attackers continued access to the compromised systems. Attractive targets for APTs include government systems, universities, and critical infrastructure.

i. Risks to Critical Infrastructure

Critical infrastructure systems are connected to many of the basics of everyday life, so vulnerabilities in these systems can create society-wide risk. Most critical infrastructure is owned and operated by the private sector, so security practices can vary significantly. In 2012, attackers reportedly compromised Telvent, a company that provides information technology services to operators of oil and gas pipelines.[6] The Telvent intruders may have stolen sensitive information like blueprints and remote access codes for oil and gas pipelines across North and South America.

Cyber threats also endanger economic infrastructure. Financial actors on Wall Street are frequently targeted with Distributed Denial of Service (DDoS) attacks. Hackers have also

---

[6] Deborah Norris Rodin, Note, *The Cybersecurity Partnership: A Proposal for Cyberthreat Information Sharing Between Contractors and the Federal Government*, 44 PUB. CONT. L.J. 505, 506 (2015).

compromised brokerage accounts to execute "hack, pump, and dump" schemes to manipulate the prices of penny stocks. In 2013, hackers compromised the Twitter account of the Associated Press and sent out a false tweet about an explosion at the White House, causing the S&P 500 to drop almost a full percentage point in value in just seconds. The Syrian Electronic Army took credit for the attack.

The critical information infrastructure underlying the Internet is another attractive target for attackers. A survey by Symantec revealed that politically-motivated cyberattacks affected approximately half of the providers of critical information infrastructure in 2010.[7] In December 2015, the media reported that unknown hackers were attempting to shut down the entire Internet by targeting DDoS attacks at vital servers. In October 2016, an unknown hacker or group of hackers successfully shut down servers belonging to Dyn, one of the major Domain Name Server (DNS) infrastructure providers. The attack on Dyn was conducted using a portion of a large botnet consisting of millions of Internet-connected devices, including CCTV cameras and digital video recorders. Some threats to information infrastructure are physical, such as the repeated incidences of vandals cutting fiber-optic cables in California. Whether physical or digital, vulnerabilities in critical information infrastructure can have national security

---

[7]   Symantec, Symantec 2010 Critical Infrastructure Protection Study: Global Results (2010).

implications due to the overlap between civilian and military networks.

With the increasing popularity of the Internet of Things, household appliances are going on-line, usually without strong security, and in many cases, with no security at all. The 2015 and 2016 attacks against Ukraine's power grid used malware that targeted critical infrastructure, but smart devices potentially offer another way to disrupt electricity. Researchers warn that eventually, hackers who have compromised a large number of "smart" major home appliances (like air conditioners and water heaters) may be able to cause enough of a surge in power consumption to cause blackouts of large geographic regions.[8]

b. THREAT CATEGORIES

To understand the scope of cybersecurity threats, one should also have a basic understanding of attack methods. There are three broad categories of cyber threats: malicious software (such as viruses, Trojan horses and worms), unauthorized remote intrusions by individuals, and denial-of-service (DoS) attacks. The line between these categories is not always clear. Some aspects of an SQL injection, which we examine later in this chapter, resemble unauthorized remote intrusions, in that this method allows the attacker to do things with the database that they are not supposed to do. When a tool has been created to

---

[8]   Andy Greenberg, *How Hacked Water Heaters Could Trigger Mass Blackouts*, WIRED (Aug. 13, 2018, 7:00 AM), https://www.wired.com/story/water-heaters-power-grid-hack-blackout/.

exploit an SQL vulnerability, it also falls into the malicious software category.

Malicious software, also called malware, comes in a wide variety of forms, including Trojan horses and rootkits. A Trojan horse is a piece of software that appears to be legitimate but that has harmful effects that can potentially include allowing malicious users to have backdoor access to the system. Symantec defines the term "rootkit" relative to Windows machines as "programs that use system hooking or modification to hide files, processes, registry keys, and other objects in order to hide programs and behaviors."[9]   Basically,   rootkits   on   Windows machines can allow attackers to do more harm before they get caught. Rootkits are also used to give an attacker an elevated level of authorization. The Stuxnet worm included a rootkit that is regarded as the first known rootkit affecting industrial control systems.

i. Botnets

Some malware is not used for the purpose of harming the target, but instead to use that computer as a tool against other targets. When a computer is controlled in this way, it is sometimes referred to as a zombie system. Zombifying malware could be used to take control of an unprotected (or under-protected) computer, making it one of thousands of computers in the same "zombie hoard" or "botnet." A botnet can be defined as "a network of computers, usually

---

[9]   Symantec, Windows Rootkit Overview (2005).

programmed for some repetitive task, under a single control mechanism."[10] The botnet master could then use the botnet to send massive amounts of spam, or order the botnet to flood an organization's website with data and requests in a Distributed Denial of Service (DDoS) attack.

Viruses that are designed to "zombify" systems might use zero-day vulnerabilities to compromise a large number of systems, but non-zero-days will likely work just as well. The widespread effectiveness of zero-day vulnerabilities is not generally necessary for building a botnet. To build a botnet, the hacker just needs to use an attack method that enough computers are vulnerable to.

ii. Denial of Service Attacks

Another category of attack is the denial of service (DoS) attack. DoS attacks are conducted by an attacker who overwhelms the targeted computer system with data and requests in order to cause the target to be unable to function. A DoS attack is an example of a cyber operation that requires multiple attacks over time, because when the attacks stop, the targeted system will recover. CERT defines DoS attacks as attacks that are intended "to prevent legitimate users of a service from using that service."[11]

---

[10]   T. Luis de Guzman, *Unleashing a Cure for the Botnet Zombie Plague: Cybertorts, Counterstrikes, and Privileges*, 59 CATH. U. L. REV. 527, 528–29 (2010).

[11]   US-CERT, Understanding Denial of Service Attacks.

As network capacity grew, attackers amplified their attacks. Distributed Denial of Service (DDoS) attacks are DoS attacks coming from a lot of computers at once. With a DDoS attack, it is harder for defenders to block the source of the "noise" that is causing the system to crash. DDoS attacks remain a serious threat in part because of the flood of Internet-connected devices in the current technology market, and the fact that a lot of these devices were not designed with security in mind. One example is the cameras and DVRs that were swept up in the Mirai botnet, which was the tool used in the DDoS attack against Dyn. Internet-connected CCTV cameras allow people to check on their homes from their smartphones anywhere in the world, but that connectivity also allowed some of those cameras to be compromised. From cameras to pedometers and refrigerators, the market is introducing many types of new Internet-connected devices. Without a focus on security, these devices are often vulnerable to being compromised and used to flood a target with data noise to make their systems crash.

But sometimes, a system may crash because too many legitimate users tried to access it at once. One case involving the federal Computer Fraud and Abuse Act (CFAA) considers this problem. In Pulte Homes, Inc. v. Laborers' Intern. Union of North America, a union undertook a campaign encouraging people to contact a builder over labor issues.[12] It was a very successful campaign, leading to phone lines and fax lines being tied up as contacts poured in.

---

[12]   648 F.3d 295 (2011).

Because of the difficulty of distinguishing between a large number of legitimate requests and a DDoS attack, DDoS attacks are difficult to criminalize effectively. In *Pulte*, the court concluded that the flood of contact attempts constituted a transmission for the purposes of one claim under the CFAA, but rejected Pulte's argument that the barrage of calls and emails amounted to access without authorization.

DDoS attacks are difficult to defend against, and can also overwhelm passive defenses and make the system more vulnerable to other attacks. These attacks are also costly for businesses. Using data collected through surveys, website security company Incapsula released a report in 2014 estimating that DDoS attacks cost a business approximately $40,000 an hour. There are significant concerns that attackers might use DDoS attacks against critical infrastructure, such as hospitals and defense infrastructure. In 2016, attackers successfully interrupted Internet access for millions of users in the United States by taking a major DNS infrastructure provider offline. Websites that used Dyn's domain name system, including famous services like Twitter and Reddit, were suddenly inaccessible. The method was a DDoS attack using the Mirai botnet, which allowed approximately 100,000 Internet of Things devices to be used as a massive weapon against the provider.

DDoS attacks have historically relied on botnets, but recent developments have shown that this is not always the case. On February 28, 2018, the popular developer platform GitHub was hit with an astronomical DDoS attack of 1.35 terabits per second, beating the previously recorded high of 1.2 terabits per second during the attack on Dyn. GitHub uses security products that can mitigate DDoS attacks, and the attack was over within about twenty minutes. The attack was an amplification attack that used memcached servers, which are a feature of the Internet that increase the speed of accessing networks and websites. When attacking GitHub, attackers spoofed the victim's IP address and sent requests to memcached servers that resulted in the servers responding with fifty times the volume of data that the attackers originally sent from the spoofed IP address.

DDoS attacks are also offered as a service, allowing less technologically savvy people to pay for an attack against their chosen target. In 2018, an international law enforcement team shut down Webstresser.org, which was thought to be the largest DDoS-for-hire website on the Internet at the time.

c.   HACKING TECHNIQUES

Software products inherently have bugs, and some of these bugs are security flaws. To exploit a security flaw, a hacker identifies a point in the code that is vulnerable to allowing outsiders to exercise some control over the system. This point is sometimes referred to as the "attack vector" because it is the path that the hacker uses to obtain unauthorized access to a system.

Over the last several years, many of the publicized attacks on private companies have involved "SQL injections," which is a very popular and effective method of hacking, especially when the goal is to steal information. SQL stands for "Structured Query Language," which is a coding language that is commonly used for managing large databases. Code might be vulnerable to an SQL injection if there is an opportunity for a user to input data that gives the system more commands or triggers the production of more information than would be produced by the expected input. An SQL injection essentially interrupts the pre-written commands and inserts new commands by using similar syntax.

An oversimplified explanation can help readers visualize this. Imagine that you have a website with a form on it. Forms allow websites to collect feedback from visitors, but are also a notoriously vulnerable feature. A computer has to execute the website's code. If a hacker knows how the website is coded, they can sometimes use web forms to trick the computer into thinking that the user input has ended, and then insert a new command that will be executed when the form is submitted. So let's say that you have a field that looks like this:

Name: [_____] *

Someone who wants to harm the website might make a few educated guesses about how the website's code is written. If they can input the right command in the same syntax that the computer is expecting

when it executes the website's code, the computer
might instead do whatever the intruder demands.
And now the potential hacker has input this:

Name: Pat)"; DROP TABLE index;-- *

If the syntax is correct and the parenthesis, quote
mark, and semi-colon are treated as the end of the
form input, this would tell the computer that the
input in the Name field was "Pat." The computer
would then move on and execute the following
command. "Drop table" is a command for deleting
part of a database. Here, if there is a section of the
database called "index," that table of data will be
deleted. Alternately, an attacker who uses this
method might insert a command that causes the
computer to display the contents of the database,
thus enabling the theft of data.

Other possible vulnerabilities include bugs in
permission settings, buffer overflow bugs, and kernel
flaws. Buffer overflow bugs are a very common target
of malware, in part because of their familiarity and
predictability. They are functionally similar to SQL
injections. Software often allocates a set amount of
space, the buffer, for user input. If the input provided
does not fit into the assigned buffer, the buffer could
overflow like a clogged sink. A hacker might include
new statements in the overflow portion that cause
something else to happen. The Heartbleed bug
affecting OpenSSL encryption software is a variation
on this type of bug, as it allowed attackers to exploit
buffer limit issues to view protected data. As with

SQL injections, a major draw of these types of attack vectors is their ability to let the intruder access non-public information. In our story, the security flaw in Compbiz's product allowed unauthorized access to databases. Buffer overflow exploits or SQL injections would thus be a likely suspect in Brian's malware.

Finding the vulnerability, like the aforementioned SQL injection or buffer overflow opportunities, is just the first step. Software vulnerabilities become dangerous when someone invests the time and energy to weaponize that vulnerability, thereby creating an exploit. Exploits can then be used maliciously, or they can be used in peaceful research. Furthermore, exploits may simply be nuisances to the computer owner because they cause infected machines to run slower, or they might be destructive and cause the corruption or deletion of important files. Security consumers may respond more ambivalently to nuisance exploits compared to destructive exploits, even though the social cost of nuisance exploits may be the same if the computer's impaired operation is because the computer is now part of a botnet.

After identifying the security flaw, the hacker might then write a tool to take advantage of this vulnerability, perhaps as a "Trojan horse" attached to something the user wants to install. Once this tool has been written, the aim is to get someone to install the tool on a system that the hacker wants to compromise. Traditionally, this has required the target to actually open an executable file; but hackers have also successfully embedded malware in word processing files and PDF files.[13] Additionally, a malicious hacker can infect website visitors who do not intentionally install anything. They might, for example, transmit a Trojan by using website coding to embed a malicious website within the website that the visitor intended to visit.[14] The black hat hacker in our story, Brian, used a malicious website to gain access to Retailco's under-protected systems.

A specific type of attack that has garnered a lot of attention recently is ransomware. Ransomware is a type of malware threat that could be devastating for a law firm. When a computer is infected with ransomware, the malware encrypts all of the files on the computer. The ransomware then displays a message for the user, directing them to pay a ransom within a certain time limit (often just a few days) or else the decryption key will be destroyed and the data will be inaccessible forever. There are some potential technical solutions, but if a company does not consistently back up their necessary files, the temptation to pay the ransom may be very strong. The FBI has even shown some ambivalence on the issue of whether victims should just pay the ransom.

Ransomware is often spread through malicious links in phishing emails, much like Brian's technique

---

[13]   Leyla Bilge & Tudor Dumitras, *Before We Knew It: An Empirical Study of Zero-Day Attacks in the Real World* 837, in PROC. ACM CONF. ON COMPUTER AND COMMUNICATIONS SECURITY (2012).

[14]   Jianwei Zhuge, Thorsten Holz, Chengyu Song, Jinpeng Guo, Xinhui Han & Wei Zou, *Studying Malicious Websites and the Underground Economy on the Chinese Web* 236–37, in MANAGING INFORMATION RISK AND THE ECONOMICS OF SECURITY (2009).

in our story, except Brian's goal was the theft of information rather than to impair the network's accessibility. Hospitals have become a very attractive target for ransomware because access to the most current and accurate information in patient files may be a literal matter of life and death. Ransomware is a threat for many other professions where immediate access to digitally stored information is essential. In 2017, a law firm sued its insurance provider, arguing that the provider had breached its contractual obligations in refusing to provide coverage for business interruption when the firm's computers were infected with ransomware and they lost access to their stored data for three months.[15]

Cryptomining malware is another growing cybersecurity threat, though its implications for infected systems may be less severe than those of ransomware. Such malware, instead of encrypting data, reallocates computer resources to "mining" cryptocurrency on behalf of some central operator, thereby directly generating profit for that operator.

d.   TECHNOLOGICAL HACKING PLUS HUMAN ERROR

A hacker targeting an institution will often need credentials to gain access. There are many possible ways of obtaining this information, but one of the most effective is arguably phishing, which primarily exploits a different type of vulnerability—the human operator. Phishing scams have long been an effective

---

[15]   Moses Afonso Ryan LTD v. Sentinel Insurance Company, No. 1:17-cv-00157 (D.R.I., filed April 21, 2017).

way to obtain access, and the fallout from these scams can be very expensive for the victims.

The FBI tracks a specific kind of phishing scam, often referred to as Business E-Mail Compromise scams or CEO impersonation scams, which have caused at least $3 billion in losses to companies since the FBI began tracking these scams in 2013.[16] BEC scams often involve criminals who spoof the identities of actual executives or actual business associates and then convince the victim to wire large amounts of money to a bank account. Such scams are generally very targeted, but there are also more general phishing attack methods that attempt to either infect a computer with malware or obtain access credentials. When one company employee falls victim to a phishing attack that also involves malware, this puts other company computers at risk. Even if the only thing the hacker obtained was that employee's credentials, this may still be enough to facilitate a large scale theft of customer information or intellectual property.

IV. THE LAW AND ECONOMICS OF SECURITY

Battles against security flaws are plagued by externality problems. Anderson and Moore keenly observe that "systems are particularly prone to failure when the person guarding them is not the person who suffers when they fail."[17] A single

---

[16]   FBI, Business E-Mail Compromise (2017).

[17]   Ross Anderson & Tyler Moore, *The Economics of Information Security*, 314 SCIENCE 610, 610 (2006).

infected computer might inconvenience its user, but the aggregate harm that it could do as part of a botnet is not a cost that the user has to bear. It is instead an externality. Incentivizing security investment can be even more difficult if the costs that the user would bear to fix the problems are greater than the user's expected loss from an attack.

In part because of potential costs, inaction in the face of security threats does not always indicate ignorance. Research by Workman in 2008 found that the general public is aware of security threats and what to do about them, but they often do not use freely available countermeasures.[18] They may instead choose to rely on investments made by others. This is possible because risks and benefits associated with cybersecurity are both shared, which may limit users' incentives for unilateral investment. This creates a free rider problem, where the individual community members aren't worried about security because they're pretty sure that other people are handling it.

So the social harm of cybersecurity is an externality not borne by the individual users, who have a more limited experience of harm. The limited harm as experienced by the individual user is, in turn, an externality not borne by the software vendor. In the course of software development, some argue that vendors are likely to focus on functionality

---

[18]   Michael Workman, William H. Bommer & Detmar Straub, *Security Lapses and the Omission of Information Security Measures: A Threat Control Model and Empirical Test*, 24 COMPUTERS IN HUMAN BEHAVIOR 2799, 2800 (2008).

more than security.[19] This may be because consumers tend to be more knowledgeable about functionality than about security. A lemons market may form when informational asymmetry leads to a reduction in the quality of the goods being sold. If consumers are not demanding secure software, the incentive lessens for developers to invest in security features, potentially leading to a lemons market for security.

The hackers themselves can also be viewed as economic actors. As illustrated in our example story, the morality and ethics of hacker behavior can vary. Wilma represents the white hat identity. She works for Securesoft and studies emerging cybersecurity threats in order to better serve Securesoft's customers. George, the freelance grey hat hacker, has an interest in identifying and demonstrating vulnerabilities, and he finds a flaw that enables database exploitation. Brian, the black hat hacker, acts for his own interests and with his own profit motives.

The best hackers are often driven to innovate by either money or prestige, the same motivations that drive people in any other profession. The annual Pwn2Own hacking competition attracts talent from all over the world, promising financial incentives and lots of bragging rights. Competitions are found outside of the private sector as well. To identify top talent, the Chinese government holds their own regional hacking competitions. Hacking is an

---

[19]   Taiwo A. Oriola, *Bugs for Sale: Legal and Ethical Proprieties of the Market in Software Vulnerabilities*, 28 J. MARSHALL J. COMPUTER & INFO. L. 451, 481 (2011).

industry with its own economy, and hackers are often rational market actors. If they can monetize their knowledge, many of them will.

There are several ways that cybersecurity knowledge can be monetized. Reputable companies all over the world offer bug bounty programs that reward researchers who identify security bugs in their products. The company will generally announce their program and provide guidelines, and bugs submitted will be fixed and the finder will be paid.

Bug bounty programs do not always work as intended. In 2016, the ride-share company Uber was contacted by a hacker who had broken into Uber's computer systems and stolen a large amount of user information. It was reported that the hacker found a password that allowed access to Uber's backup files on a remote server. The password was found in a file stored on Github, a website popular with software developers who want to share their code. The hacker who obtained the data demanded payment in exchange for the stolen data. Instead of reporting the extortion demand to the police, or reporting the data breach to anyone, Uber employees routed the hacker's demand through the bug bounty program and paid the hacker with the condition that the data be deleted.

Apart from bug bounties, there are other ways of monetizing vulnerability information. In what is sometimes referred to as the grey market, companies like Zerodium pay large sums of money for zero-day exploits. Unlike bug bounties, buyers in the grey market often do not use the knowledge to fix the underlying vulnerability, and instead might make those exploits available for purchase by governments. The stockpiling of zero days by governments is currently a wide open area in law and policy, and many in the private sector have become very concerned about the practice. In 2016, a group called Shadow Brokers announced that it had stolen a huge cache of zero-day exploits from the National Security Administration (NSA). In 2017, the devastating WannaCry attack utilized the EternalBlue exploit developed by the NSA and leaked by Shadow Brokers to cause massive disruption in a worldwide ransomware attack.

As there is a grey market that helps to supply governments with knowledge of security vulnerabilities, so too is there a black market designed to provide these services to other buyers who are willing to pay. The black market for vulnerability information, especially zero-day exploits, is often buried in darknet forums, accessible only through highly secure web browsing methods, where sellers are paid in cryptocurrency.

CHAPTER 3

RESPONDING TO CYBER THREATS

Okay, cyber threats are a big deal. What can we do about it? Broadly, approaches to cyber defense can be categorized using the Three Ds: Defend, Deter, Deescalate. Defending means to have the means to block attempted attacks, such as through firewalls and antivirus products. Deterrence is primarily considered from the perspective of the attacker. What would convince them that the risk is not enough to justify their possible reward? Deterrence can work by punishing the attacker, but deterrence by denial is also possible. Deescalation is about making sure that systems are resilient and can recover quickly from an incident.

There are a number of technologies that can improve defense, from the aforementioned firewalls and antivirus products to intrusion detection systems, traceback methods, and honey pots that are designed to lure attackers in order to learn more about them and their methods. Legal developments might also include requirements for security practices. Rhode Island, for example, requires risk-based information security programs for entities that handle the personal information of state residents.[1]

Deterrence is ultimately about discouraging bad actors. During the Cold War, mutually assured destruction was the main deterrent against nuclear strikes. Criminal laws and international cybercrime

---

[1]   R.I. Gen. Laws § 11–49.3–2.

treaties offer some potential deterrent effect under the deterrence-by-punishment paradigm. Strong defensive technologies can support deterrence-by-denial.

Deescalation is about getting back to normal. Deescalation strategies focusing on improving resilience can include drills to prepare staff for cybersecurity incidents. Audits can improve resilience by identifying organizational issues and quantifying available resources.

Of these three, deterrence is perhaps the most complicated. Cybercrime presents new challenges to law enforcement, with perpetrators who are little more than shadows because of the difficulty of tying a specific person to a specific computer at the time of an attack.

There have been many improvements in cybercrime fighting in recent years. One frequently used tool is website takedowns. Investigators have taken down many websites that were used to coordinate illegal activities. Webstresser.org was thought to be the largest DDoS-for-hire website on the Internet before the domain was seized by Europol in April 2018. In February 2018, the Department of Justice announced an indictment of individuals responsible for InFraud, a popular Internet forum for dealing in fraudulent financial information. The InFraud website was also shut down by authorities. InFraud was dedicated to carding, and was organized around a large discussion forum.[2] Carding typically involves financial fraud committed using stolen credentials. The prosecution of InFraud is perhaps the first major example of an online discussion forum being categorized as a criminal organization under the Racketeer Influenced and Corrupt Organizations Act (RICO).

Establishing a website's legal liability is difficult in many situations. Under Section 230 of the Communications Decency Act (CDA), a website owner is not responsible for what their users write. Section 230(c)(1) states that "No provider or user of an interactive computer service shall be treated as the publisher or speaker of any information provided by another information content provider." This provision has been read to give website owners a broad immunity from liability as long as the website owner does not help in the development of unlawful content.[3] The Ninth Circuit found no CDA immunity in a situation where a website asked users a series of questions that could be used to discriminate between possible roommate matches, because the questions "contribute[ ] materially to the alleged illegality of the conduct."[4] That case involved the website

---

[2]   Press Release, U.S. Dep't of Just., Thirty-six Defendants Indicted for Alleged Roles in Transnational Criminal Organization Responsible for More than $530 Million in Losses from Cybercrimes (Feb. 7, 2018), *available at* https://www.justice.gov/opa/pr/thirty-six-defendants-indicted-alleged-roles-transnational-criminal-organization-responsible.

[3]   J.S. v. Village Voice Media Holdings, LLC, 184 Wash. 2d 95 (Wash. 2015).

[4]   Fair Hous. Council of San Fernando Valley v. Roommates.com, LLC, 521 F.3d 1157, 1168 (9th Cir. 2008).

Roommates.com, and the court concluded that in asking the additional questions, the website acted as an information content provider instead of an interactive computer service.

In 2018, Congress enacted FOSTA-SESTA, a bill package designed to combat online sex trafficking. FOSTA-SESTA adds Section 2421A to Chapter 117 of the United States Code. The new Section 2421A creates an exception to Section 230 immunity by declaring that website publishers are responsible for third party ads for prostitution. Under Section 2421A, interactive computer services become criminally liable if they operate "with the intent to promote or facilitate the prostitution of another person." Congress was driven to pass FOSTA-SESTA because of a perceived gap in the law that blocked the prosecution of the owners of websites that allowed ads for adult services. The specific target of FOSTA-SESTA was Backpage, a successful classified ad service where a lot of the customers were sex workers. The Department of Justice surprised the media when they managed to seize Backpage.com shortly after FOSTA-SESTA passed but before the law went into effect, leading some to wonder if the new law was necessary. The stick of liability thus has been used in multiple contexts for deterring certain behaviors online. In shutting down websites and seizing resources, law enforcement hopes to deter these kinds of online activities.

Policymakers often respond to increases in crime by enhancing sentences, but studies suggest that increased sentences do little to actually reduce crime.[5] Instead, what might happen is that the increased punishments merely increase what Professor Herbert Packer called the crime tariff, which allows criminals to charge more for their illegal services due to the risk of being caught.[6]

There are also theories about the potential deterrent value of hacking back against the hackers, but self-defense online is, at best, a legally grey area. Deterrence-by-denial is legally fine, but it relies on consistent use of strong security practices. While attackers might be deterred from targeting one well-protected firm because of the futility of doing so, unless all possible targets are protected to the same extent, the attacker needs only to keep looking for a weak link.

This is not to say that any attempts at defense will be for nothing. There are a number of security firms available to consult with about network security practices. Law enforcement agencies cooperate across national borders to address cybercrime threats, leading to more effective deterrence.

Some industries also self-regulate on matters of data security. The payment card industry has a data security standard called PCI-DSS, and merchants must comply with these terms to accept credit cards at their establishments. For over twenty years, TrustArc (formerly TRUSTe) has offered

---

[5]   Steven N. Durlauf & Daniel S. Nagin, *Imprisonment and Crime: Can Both Be Reduced?*, 10 CRIMINOLOGY AND PUB. POL'Y 13 (2011).

[6]   Herbert Packer, *The Crime Tariff*, 33 AM. SCHOLAR 551 (1964).

certifications for websites to signal responsible data privacy practices. However, in 2014, the FTC found that TRUSTe failed to conduct the annual recertifications as promised in over 1,000 separate incidences between 2006 and 2013.[7]

Some have called for public private partnerships to improve cybersecurity, believing that cooperation between the government and private sector can keep all parties informed of emerging trends. An attorney interested in learning more about such collaborations in a particular industry could look for a relevant information sharing and analysis center (ISAC). There are ISACs for the financial services sector, the communications sector, and the automotive sector, among others.

---

[7] Press Release, Federal Trade Commission, TRUSTe Settles FTC Charges It Deceived Consumers Through Its Privacy Seal Program (Nov. 17, 2014), *available at* http://www.ftc.gov/ news-events/press-releases/2014/11/truste-settles-ftc-charges-it-deceived-consumers-through-its.

CHAPTER 4

COMPUTER FRAUD AND ABUSE ACT

We turn now from more general discussions of cybersecurity and the law to specific statutes proscribing cyber misconduct. In the United States, the most prominent statute is the federal Computer Fraud and Abuse Act (CFAA). Congress enacted a version of the CFAA in 1984 and substantially amended it in 1986. Between 1986 and 2018, the CFAA has been amended nine times, with the most recent amendments having been made in 2008. The CFAA broadly prohibits unauthorized activity on a protected computer, as well as a few other offenses. For some provisions, the prohibition on unauthorized activity extends both to activity without authorization and activity that exceeds authorized access.

The entirety of the CFAA is found in 18 U.S.C. § 1030. Section 1030(a) sets forth the specific actions that are prohibited. The following table summarizes the offenses under the CFAA as well as the sentencing for a first offense.

Offense	Section	Maximum sentence for first offense
Obtaining national security information, without (or exceeding) authorization	(a)(1)	10 years
Accessing a computer and obtaining information, without (or exceeding) authorization	(a)(2)	1 or 5 years (with aggravating factors)
Access of a government computer without authorization	(a)(3)	1 year
Accessing a computer to defraud and obtain value, without (or exceeding) authorization	(a)(4)	5 years

Intentionally damaging by knowing transmission, without authorization	(a)(5)(A)	1 or 10 years up to life (with aggravating factors)
Recklessly damaging by intentional access, without authorization	(a)(5)(B)	1 or 5 years (with aggravating factors)
Causing damage and loss by intentional access, without authorization	(a)(5)(C)	1 year
Trafficking in passwords	(a)(6)	1 year
Extortion involving computers	(a)(7)	5 years

Table 1:   CFAA Provisions

In the previous chapter's dramatic tale of cybersecurity intrigue, Brian the Black Hat tricked a Retailco employee into clicking a phishing link. Brian then used the compromised computer to obtain information from the company's customer databases. His actions clearly violate section 1030(a)(2), which prohibits obtaining information without authorization. He also violated 1030(a)(5)(A), because he transmitted malicious code to the target machine. Depending on Brian's purposes for downloading the database, there may also be a charge under 1030(a)(4). Moreover, Brian's actions might also have violated 1030(a)(5)(B) or 1030(a)(5)(C) if his actions caused any loss of data to Retailco, or if his actions resulted in service interruptions for Retailco or their customers. That turns on the CFAA's definition of damage, which is discussed in a later section.

I.   CRIME AND PUNISHMENT

The table above notes that aggravating factors can increase the sentence for a first offense. Aggravating factors vary with the provision violated. Violations of 1030(a)(2) have a maximum sentence of five years if the offense was committed for "commercial advantage or private financial gain," if it was committed "in furtherance of any criminal or tortious act," or if the value of the information exceeds $5,000. Violations of 1030(a)(5)(A) and (B) have higher maximum sentences if the violation caused over $5,000 in aggregated loss, affected medical information, created a threat to public safety, damaged ten or more computers during a one year period, or if the damaged computers included computers used by the United States government "in furtherance of the administration of justice, national defense, or national security." 1030(c)(4)(E) and (c)(4)(F) go further for violations of (a)(5)(A). If the intentional damage by transmission caused serious bodily injury, the maximum sentence is twenty years.

If the violation caused death, a life sentence becomes the maximum possible sentence for a first violation.

For all of the provisions, subsequent violations also enhance potential sentences. Subsequent convictions for 1030(a)(1), (a)(5)(A), or (a)(5)(B) carry a maximum sentence of twenty years. For all other provisions, the maximum sentence for subsequent convictions is ten years.

II. WHAT IS A COMPUTER?

The CFAA defines a computer as "an electronic, magnetic, optical, electrochemical, or other high speed data processing device performing logical, arithmetic, or storage functions." Courts have found a wide range of devices to be "computers" under the CFAA. However, most of the provisions of the CFAA require the computer to be something more specific. Originally, the CFAA required the affected system to be a "Federal interest computer." In the 1986 version of the CFAA, the term "Federal interest computer" was defined as including only the computers used in committing an offense, or a computer that is used by financial institutions or the United States government. A few years later, the CFAA was amended to replace "Federal interest computer" with "protected computer." Under the current definition, a "protected computer" could be a financial institution's computer, a computer used by the United States government, or any computer that is used in or affects interstate commerce or communication.

The last category seemingly includes any computer with an Internet connection. During the process of amending the CFAA in 2008, Representative Scott of Virginia advocated for using access to the Internet to satisfy the "protected computer" definition's requirements of effects on interstate commerce or communication.[1] This interpretation from legislative history is also supported by a 2007 case in the 8th Circuit, United States v. Trotter.[2] In *Trotter*, the defendant attempted to argue that "protected computers" should not include the computers of non-profit organizations. The court disagreed, quoting an earlier court that said of the CFAA, "once the computer is used in interstate commerce, Congress has the power to protect it." As the Information Age progressed, the CFAA has grown to encompass any tool that accesses the Internet, including laptops, smartphones, iPads, and Internet of Things devices.

III. CIVIL SUITS

Courts have consistently interpreted the CFAA's language very broadly to prohibit a wide variety of acts, perhaps in part because Congress has consistently broadened the CFAA every time it was amended over the last 30 years. Today, a review of cases that include claims based on the CFAA finds a large number of incidents where an employee took information from an employer's computers before or after leaving the company. Such cases also often

---

[1]   154 Cong. Rec. H8075-01 (Sep. 15, 2008).

[2]   478 F.3d 918 (8th Cir. 2007).

involve claims of trade secret theft. This is in addition to the many criminal cases filed.

While the CFAA is primarily a criminal statute, section (g) of the CFAA creates a cause of action to allow victims to sue the violator for compensatory damages or equitable relief. Civil actions under 1030(g) are limited to conduct involving one of the first five factors listed in section 1030(c)(4)(A)(i). Those factors are the aggravating factors provided for violations of section 1030(a)(5)(B). Remember that 1030(a)(5)(B) prohibits intentional unauthorized access that recklessly causes damage. Civil suits under 1030(g) are often pled based on violations of section 1030(a)(5)(B), but courts have also permitted civil suits based on violations of other provisions. This includes (a)(2)'s provision for accessing and obtaining information, (a)(4)'s access with the intent to defraud, and (a)(5)(A)'s transmission that causes damage, as long as the aggravating factors are present.

Section 1030(c)(4)(A)(i) actually has six factors, but 1030(g) only references the first five as providing grounds for a civil suit. The sixth factor, causing damage that affects ten or more computers in a one year period, is conspicuously absent. All six factors and the importance of five of them to civil suits were added in their current form in Public Law 110–326, the Former Vice President Protection Act (H.R. 5938). The legislative history indicates that sixth factor about damage to ten or more computers was added to address the threat of spyware. It is unclear why Congress did not conclude that damage to ten or more computers should be enough to support a civil suit under section 1030(g).

For a brief period in the late 1990s, plaintiffs attempted to apply the CFAA to impose liability on software producers whose products caused damage to customer computers. One such case is Shaw v. Toshiba America Information Systems, where the flaw in issue was faulty microcode.[3] In 2001, Section 1030(g) was amended to not allow civil actions to be brought for the negligent design or manufacture of computer software, hardware, or firmware. On the other hand, Section 1030(g) has repeatedly been interpreted to provide recourse for employers with disloyal employees, in addition to victims of cyberattacks. Congress has not amended the CFAA to limit liability in the context of employment conflicts the way they did for manufacturers, so it can be assumed that for now these causes of action fall within Congress's intent. The history of the CFAA thus shows an ongoing quest to refine questions of liability.

IV. THE CFAA, DEFEND TRADE SECRETS ACT, AND ECONOMIC ESPIONAGE ACT

Businesses often rely on intellectual property protections to secure a competitive advantage. Trade secrets have historically been a state law issue for civil actions, though that changed in 2016 with the passage of the Defend Trade Secrets Act (codified at 18 U.S.C. § 1836). Prior to DTSA, the federal

---

[3]   91 F. Supp. 2d 926 (E.D. Tex. 1999).

Economic Espionage Act addressed trade secret theft, but the language emphasized government enforcement. After the DTSA, trade secret owners have a federal cause of action for trade secret misappropriation "if the trade secret is related to a product or service used in, or intended for use in, interstate or foreign commerce."

As noted above, the civil provisions of the CFAA are frequently used against disloyal employees who stole a company's trade secrets. It is not known yet what impact the DTSA will have on the number of trade secret-related claims brought under Section 1030(g) of the CFAA. To the extent that the CFAA was being used for federal jurisdiction, litigants might instead prefer the more intentional trade secret protection of the DTSA. As the rest of this chapter makes clear, legal questions abound concerning the CFAA, especially concerning authorization and damages.

Before passage of the DTSA, the Economic Espionage Act just provided fines and prison sentences for trade secret theft. It was not, then, a viable option for civil litigants. The CFAA thus provided a federal complement to the EEA by allowing for civil litigation over improperly obtained information. Complicating matters, neither of the two statutes were written with the other in mind. The EEA's language focuses on trade secrets, compared to the CFAA's general focus on information. Another sign of the different goals of the two is what type of behavior is addressed. The CFAA is limited to the medium of computers, while violations of the EEA can involve any method of trade secret theft.

They both, however, address actions benefiting a foreign government. In the EEA, this is Section 1831, which specifically addresses trade secret theft that will benefit a foreign government. In the CFAA, this is similar to the first violation enumerated in Section 1030(a)(1). That section addresses the unauthorized acquisition of information that requires "protection from improper disclosure" or that is "restricted data," and then subsequent action or inaction involving that information. Such actions are covered by the CFAA if the information "could be used to the injury of the United States, or to the advantage of any foreign nation."

Though the DTSA has shifted the civil liability paradigm, it has left the regulatory paradigm largely unchanged, with the EEA still providing criminal penalties for actions related to trade secret misappropriation. Some crimes are based on the activity's usefulness for committing future crimes. Other crimes look downstream to future uses of the fruits of the criminal act. The CFAA includes an upstream crime in Section 1030(a)(6) by criminalizing the act of trafficking in passwords or similar access-related information. The EEA includes a downstream crime by criminalizing the act of receiving information that one knows to have been illegally acquired. The way this upstream/ downstream distinction arises in state cybercrime laws is addressed in a future chapter.

V. CIRCUIT SPLITS

The CFAA is the subject of significant disagreements between jurisdictions. The first major substantive split concerns what types of injuries count towards the damage and loss requirements of the statute. The second substantive split concerns the meaning of authorization and when authorization has been lost.

Many of the cases that will be discussed in this chapter concern trade secret misappropriation. This text is primarily concerned with security and privacy, but it is worthwhile to note that the CFAA has frequently been used to buttress claims of trade secret misappropriation and unfair competition. Again, the future application of the CFAA to trade secrets in a post-DTSA world is still unclear, but these cases nonetheless provide essential analysis of the CFAA. In part because of evidentiary issues, prosecutions for actual cybercrimes are not very common, and prosecutions that result in published opinions are even less so. The civil cases brought under Section 1030(g), therefore, provide helpful guidance about the language of the statute.

a.   DAMAGE AND LOSS

Section 1030(a)(5) is often central in cases pertaining to computer intrusions that cause damage. "Damage" is defined in 1030(e) as "any impairment to the integrity or availability of data, a program, a system, or information." When evaluating this definition, courts have often held that permanent file deletion counts as damage. Such was the case in International Airport Centers v. Citrin,[4] where the defendant used a secure-erasure program to permanently delete files to hide his questionable activities.

What is less clear, on the other hand, is whether information theft alone counts as damage. A majority of jurisdictions hold that it does not. For example, the district court in Garelli Wong & Associates, Inc. v. Nichols held that the theft of trade secrets via unauthorized computer access was not damage under the CFAA.[5] What's more, the *Garelli Wong* court held that pleadings under the CFAA must establish both damage *and* loss, even though 1030(g) merely requires damage *or* loss.

On the issue of damage under the CFAA, a minority of courts have held that "impairment to the integrity" of data can include information theft. In Shurgard Storage Centers, Inc. v. Safeguard Self Storage, Inc.,[6] the district court stated that "[t]he word "integrity" in the context of data necessarily contemplates maintaining the data in a protected state." The court further concludes that the legislative history of the 1996 amendments to the CFAA supports this interpretation.

Other circuits that have considered this point have typically disagreed with the *Shurgard* court, but the

---

[4]   440 F.3d 418 (7th Cir. 2006).

[5]   551 F. Supp. 2d 704 (N.D. Ill. 2008).

[6]   119 F. Supp. 2d 1121 (W.D. Wash. 2000).

Ninth Circuit has not yet ruled on this question and so *Shurgard* still has precedential value in the Western District of Washington where it was decided. In *Garelli Wong & Associates*, the court declined to follow the *Shurgard* case, asserting that subsequent legislative history superseded this reading of the damage definition. The reasoning for this conclusion is unclear, as subsequent amendments have not narrowed the definition of damage as it existed when it was added in the 1996 amendments, nor have subsequent amendments defined integrity.

"Loss" is defined in Section 1030(e) as: "any reasonable cost to any victim, including the cost of responding to an offense, conducting a damage assessment, and restoring the data, program, system, or information to its condition prior to the offense, and any revenue lost, cost incurred, or other consequential damages incurred because of interruption of service." Loss thus refers to costs incurred as a result of damage, but lost revenue is only considered when it results from a service interruption. The cost of hiring a computer forensics consultant to determine the extent of harm, therefore, could fairly be considered a loss under the CFAA. On the other hand, if the alleged CFAA offense involved a former employee stealing trade secrets and going to work for a competitor, it is doubtful that lost revenue resulting from that betrayal will be considered a loss under the CFAA.[7]

Another case originating in Washington state, Pacific Aerospace & Electronics v. Taylor, adopted a broad interpretation of loss.[8] The *Pacific Aerospace & Electronics* case also relied on a First Circuit case, EF Cultural Travel v. Explorica, to conclude that "any losses stemming from the unauthorized conduct are recoverable." *Explorica* concerned a company that used scraping software to collect data from a competitor's website.[9] The plaintiff in *Explorica* alleged loss "consisting of reduced business, harm to its goodwill, and the cost of diagnostic measures it incurred to evaluate possible harm to EF's systems."

The concepts of damage and loss become more complicated in the CFAA's civil provision in Section 1030(g). The exact language that creates confusion is:

> Any person who suffers damage or loss by reason of a violation of this section may maintain a civil action against the violator to obtain compensatory damages and injunctive relief or other equitable relief. A civil action for a violation of this section may be brought only if the conduct involves 1 of the factors set forth in

---

[7]   Am. Family Mut. Ins. Co. v. Rickman, 554 F. Supp. 2d 766 (N.D. Ohio 2008). *But see* CoStar Realty Info., Inc. v. Field, 612 F. Supp. 2d 660 (D. Md. 2009).

[8]   295 F. Supp. 2d 1205 (E.D. Wash. 2003).

[9]   EF Cultural Travel v. Explorica, 274 F.3d 577 (1st Cir. 2001).

subclauses [5] (I), (II), (III), (IV), or (V) of subsection (c)(4)(A)(i).

Shurgard is a 1030(g) case, as are most of the cases that have criticized *Shurgard*. The referenced subsection states:

(c) The punishment for an offense under subsection (a) or (b) of this section is. . . .

(4)

(A) except as provided in subparagraphs (E) and (F), a fine under this title, imprisonment for not more than 5 years, or both, in the case of—

(i) an offense under subsection (a)(5)(B), which does not occur after a conviction for another offense under this section, if the offense caused (or, in the case of an attempted offense, would, if completed, have caused)—

(I) loss to 1 or more persons during any 1-year period (and, for purposes of an investigation, prosecution, or other proceeding brought by the United States only, loss resulting from a related course of conduct affecting 1 or more other protected computers) aggregating at least $5,000 in value;

(II) the modification or impairment, or potential modification or impairment, of the medical examination, diagnosis, treatment, or care of 1 or more individuals;

(III) physical injury to any person;

(IV) a threat to public health or safety;

(V) damage affecting a computer used by or for an entity of the United States Government in furtherance of the administration of justice, national defense, or national security; or

(VI) damage affecting 10 or more protected computers during any 1-year period

In addition to the omission of (VI) noted above, 1030(g) also omits Section (c)(4)(A)(ii), which applies to attempted offenses. This indicates that 1030(g) suits cannot be brought if an offense was attempted but not completed.

The factor most often relied upon by litigants in 1030(g) litigation is 1030(c)(4)(A)(i)(I). That factor is "loss to 1 or more persons during any 1-year period . . . aggregating at least $5,000 in value."

The resulting debate, which is not yet settled, concerns whether the definition of damage includes information theft, and if it does, when such damage is enough for the "damage or loss" provision of Section 1030(g). In such a situation, is it possible for information theft to result in economic damages other than lost revenue?

b.   AUTHORIZATION

At its core, the CFAA is about control of information. Under the CFAA, liability attaches when control is exercised by someone who is not supposed to have control. Most of the provisions address actions that affect computers owned by someone else. The CFAA is ultimately about property crime. If I spray paint my own house, that's fine. If my neighbor spray paints my house without my permission, that's vandalism. But distinguishing physical property is comparatively easy. Permission issues in computer cases include a lot of ambiguities. Because of this, authorization under the CFAA can be a minefield for practitioners.

Authorization is central to liability under the CFAA, and is the subject of another circuit split. Some courts have characterized the split as being between a narrow view and a broad view of what it means to have, lose, or exceed authorization under the CFAA. The Seventh Circuit adopted the broad characterization in International Airport Centers, L.L.C. v. Citrin, drawing on agency law to conclude that an employee lost authorization when the employee violated his duty of loyalty to his employer. In United States v. John,[10] the Fifth Circuit applied an "intended use analysis" to conclude that the defendant exceeded authorization when she used her work computer to collect information for fraudulent purposes. Similarly, in United States v. Rodriguez, the Eleventh Circuit held that an employee of the

---

[10]   United States v. John, 597 F.3d 263 (2010).

Social Security Administration exceeded authorized access when he used his work computer to look up personal information about women he knew.[11] Public websites have also been subject to analysis based on authorization. In 2001, the First Circuit decided EF Cultural Travel BV v. Explorica, Inc., concluding that by using a scraping program designed with input from a former employee of the plaintiff, the defendant's use of plaintiff's website exceeded authorized access.[12]

The narrow characterization, on the other hand, often emphasizes the CFAA's focus on hacking. Courts that adopt the narrow view are unlikely to find a CFAA violation based on mere misappropriation by an employee. There are several criminal cases where the narrow view was adopted and which focused on statutory interpretation and the rule of lenity. In 2012, the Ninth Circuit decided United States v. Nosal,[13] concluding that the authorization language in the CFAA applied to access restrictions and not use restrictions.

In a jurisdiction that follows the precedent set by the 2012 *Nosal* decision, a defendant who has authorization to access a computer and who then misappropriates data on that computer has not lost his authorization by virtue of his tortious intent. This approach was adopted by the Second Circuit in

---

[11]   628 F.3d 1258 (11th Cir. 2010).

[12]   EF Cultural Travel v. Explorica, 274 F.3d 577 (1st Cir. 2001).

[13]   United States v. Nosal, 676 F.3d 854 (9th Cir. 2012).

United States v. Valle,[14] a case that has many parallels with United States v. Rodriguez. In both *Valle* and *Rodriguez*, a government employee used his access to information about citizens in order to collect sensitive information about specific people that he knew. But whereas the Eleventh Circuit held that misuse of information collected through authorized access was a violation of the CFAA, the Second Circuit adopted the narrow formulation and concluded that there was no such violation. In so holding, the *Valle* court emphasized that the government's reading of the CFAA could criminalize day-to-day activities, and declined to "uphold a highly problematic interpretation of a statute merely because the Government promises to use it responsibly."

The narrow characterization has also been adopted in civil suits. Before *Nosal*, the Ninth Circuit decided LVRC Holdings LLC v. Brekka,[15] which explored the question of whether an employee acted without authorization when he emailed confidential documents to his personal email address. In *Brekka*, the Ninth Circuit explicitly repudiated the Seventh Circuit's conclusion in *Citrin* that authorization is lost through disloyal actions. The Fourth Circuit adopted the reasoning of *Brekka* in WEC Carolina Energy Solutions LLC v. Miller.[16] Like many civil suits under the CFAA, *WEC Carolina* also arose in the employment context. The court in *WEC Carolina*

---

[14]   807 F.3d 508 (2d Cir. 2015).

[15]   581 F.3d 1127 (9th Cir. 2009).

[16]   687 F.3d 199 (4th Cir. 2012).

concluded that an employee would exceed authorized access when he "uses his access to obtain or alter information that falls outside the bounds of his approved access." Misuse of information that the employee was authorized to access, however, was not covered by the CFAA under their reading.

Though five CFAA counts were dismissed from the *Nosal* case in 2012,[17] Nosal was ultimately convicted of violating the CFAA. This was based on Nosal's use of someone else's password when his access to the database was taken away. This, according to the court, was unauthorized access. Nosal and others had used the login information for Nosal's former assistant in order to continue to obtain confidential information after their own access was revoked. *Nosal* went to the Ninth Circuit again in 2016, where the court affirmed Nosal's conviction.[18] Central to the Ninth Circuit's reasoning were the defendant's efforts to circumvent access restrictions. The court emphasized, however, that circumvention of a technological access barrier is not necessary to show that someone lacked authorization. In 2017, the Supreme Court decided not to grant certiorari in the case of United States v. Nosal, so the Ninth Circuit's ruling on authorization and circumvention stands.

In the past, the Department of Justice has argued that if a user of social media violates the service's terms of use, subsequent actions by the user are without authorization. A common argument in favor

---

[17]   United States v. Nosal, 676 F.3d 854 (9th Cir. 2012).

[18]   United States v. Nosal, 844 F.3d 1024 (9th Cir. 2016).

of the narrow view of authorization is that using private computer use policies and end user license agreements to determine if a crime has been committed gives these private contracts too much power. Several cases, including United States v. Drew,[19] Continental Group v. KW Property Management,[20] and Modis, Inc. v. Bardelli,[21] emphasized contract language to determine whether an individual exceeded their authorized access. The contracts in issue were, respectively, a website terms of service agreement, a set of computer access policies, and an employment agreement.

VI. SPECIFIC CASES

In this section, we examine three specific criminal prosecutions under the CFAA. The first, United States v. Morris,[22] is a Second Circuit case that is a landmark case in two senses. First, it was the first indictment under the CFAA, and second, it concerned the first known Internet worm. The second case, United States v. Auernheimer,[23] was decided by the Third Circuit in 2014. Auernheimer is significant because it shows the evolving ideas of what a CFAA violation entails. The third case, United States v. Nosal, is a Ninth Circuit case applying CFAA to questions of misappropriation of confidential information.

---

[19]   259 F.R.D. 449 (C.D. Cal. 2009).

[20]   622 F.Supp.2d 1357 (S.D. Fla. 2009).

[21]   531 F.Supp.2d 314 (D. Conn. 2008).

[22]   928 F.2d 504 (2d Cir. 1991).

[23]   748 F.3d 525 (3d Cir. 2014).

a.   UNITED STATES V. MORRIS (2D CIR. 1991)

Morris was the first federal prosecution under the CFAA. The defendant was Robert Morris, a computer science graduate student at Cornell, who wrote and released a computer worm that exploited vulnerabilities of computer networks. It was through the Morris case that we derive our current understanding that the intent requirement of the CFAA, unless stated otherwise, primarily applies to access. The emphasis is on whether you intended to access the computer, not whether you intended to act without authorization.

It is worth noting that not only was Robert Morris the first person indicted under the CFAA, his Morris worm was also the first known worm released on the Internet. Morris has stated that the original purpose of the worm was to estimate the size of the Internet. Unfortunately, the more copies of the worm that were on a computer, the slower the computer ran, until the computer was unusable. This effect has often been categorized as an unintended consequence. However, questions still remain. If Morris did not intend for the worm to cause damage, why release it on the MIT network instead of on the Cornell network where he was actually a student?

Regardless of intent, the worm did in fact cause disruption. If nothing else, the Morris prosecution represents the application of the CFAA to computer security actions driven by curiosity.

b.   UNITED STATES V. AUERNHEIMER
(3D CIR. 2014)

A chance discovery of a security flaw led to United States v. Auernheimer. Daniel Spitler, an online acquaintance of Andrew Auernheimer's, was the defendant's co-conspirator. The chance discovery occurred in 2010 when Spitler was trying to figure out how to obtain one of the $30 per month unlimited data plans that AT&T made available to iPad owners—without actually purchasing an iPad. In the course of Spitler's efforts, he discovered that accessing a user account with an iPad browser required a nineteen or twenty digit Integrated Circuit Card Identifier (ICC-ID), and this number was tied to the device. Accessing the AT&T login page from an iPad (or a spoofed iPad browser) led to the user's email address being automatically populated into the user identifier field, because the browser detected the ICC-ID and redirected the user to a login page with the ICC-ID displayed in the URL. Guessing that ICC-ID numbers may be sequential, Spitler added one to the final number, and the browser populated a login page listing the email address of another iPad owner.

Spitler then contacted Auernheimer, and the two developed a program that would automatically increment ICC-ID numbers and record the email addresses produced. This way, the two discovered 114,000 email addresses of iPad owners. While the information was limited to email addresses, there were some very high profile individuals whose email addresses were revealed, making this potentially a very valuable database. The two conspirators publicized their findings by contacting members of the media.

A prosecution soon followed in a New Jersey federal court. Spitler pled guilty and was placed on probation because of his display of remorse. Auernheimer went to trial on charges of conspiracy to violate the CFAA and the federal identity theft law, and upon conviction was sentenced to 41 months in prison. On appeal, the Third Circuit vacated the conviction on venue grounds. Neither Auernheimer nor Spitler were in New Jersey at the time of the violation, nor were any of the affected systems, and while some of the people whose information was leaked probably did live in New Jersey, the court did not think that was enough. The court considered whether any of the essential conduct elements of the charged offenses took place in New Jersey, and concluded that the essential conduct was absent from that jurisdiction.

Criminal practitioners may also want to take note of a different aspect of *Auernheimer*. On appeal, the Third Circuit acknowledged that Auernheimer's offense was elevated from a misdemeanor to a felony because of the prosecution's strategic inclusion of a charge of violating New Jersey's computer crime statute. One of the elements of the CFAA's sentencing provisions allows for elevating a violation of section 1030(a)(2)(C) to a felony if the violation occurs in furtherance of a violation of state law. New Jersey's computer crime law is similar to the CFAA, so by allowing state law to provide an enhancement qualification for a CFAA sentence, the offense essentially enhances itself. The appellate court did not address the dynamic of using a state cybercrime statute to enhance a CFAA sentence.

c.   UNITED STATES V. NOSAL (9TH CIR.)

David Nosal was a regional director for Korn Ferry, an executive search firm. After being passed over for a promotion, he started making plans with other firm employees to leave the firm and start a competing business. To facilitate this, they wanted to copy content from Korn Ferry's database, Searcher. The firm considered Searcher and its content to be proprietary and confidential. Access to Searcher was password-protected and was restricted to employees. Nosal and his cohorts downloaded some content from Searcher while they still had access with their own passwords. After they left their jobs and their access rights were revoked, they continued to access Searcher by using a password belonging to a current Korn Ferry employee.

In 2012, the Ninth Circuit held that downloading information from Searcher while still employed did not "exceed authorized access" under the CFAA. Following that appeal, Nosal was convicted of several remaining charges, including violations of the CFAA and the Economic Espionage Act. Nosal appealed the conviction, arguing among other things that the government's reading of the CFAA would criminalize password-sharing. The Ninth Circuit affirmed the conviction in 2016. The majority concluded that the issue was not password-sharing, but rather the revocation of access and the efforts to circumvent that revocation. Password-sharing was merely the tool that enabled the circumvention. Judge Reinhardt dissented from the 2016 opinion, warning that the majority "los[t] sight of the anti-hacking purpose of the CFAA."

Taken together, the 2012 *Nosal* opinion and the 2016 *Nosal* opinion stand for the proposition that a person does not exceed authorized access if they use their own passwords to access a computer and then misappropriate information contained therein, but an intentional revocation of authorization cannot be subverted by other means.

CHAPTER 5

STATE CYBERCRIME LAWS

The CFAA provides a federal framework for cybercrime, and all fifty states have additional cybercrime laws in their state codes. This chapter examines how state approaches to cybercrime can vary. There is not currently a uniform cyber incident law in the United States, and the Model Penal Code also lacks any meaningful discussion of the growing threats posed by cybercrime.

The technology that enables the worst incidents of cybercrime has exploded in recent years, but in spite of efforts in Congress, the CFAA has not been amended since 2008. Some states have also been slow to update their cybercrime laws to keep up with expanding threats, but the majority of states have amended their cybercrime laws at least once between 2012 and 2018.

That these laws have changed so much over the last decade already sets cybercrime apart from older categories of crimes like larceny and arson. The important thing is that, when litigation becomes technologically complex, lawyers should keep in mind the evolving nature of cybercrime laws. Jurisdiction, for example, can be a thorny topic in cybercrime prosecutions and civil litigation because of the amorphous reality of country and state borders on the Internet. There are twenty-five states that explicitly address jurisdiction and venue issues as part of their cybercrime laws, or in separate provisions that reference the cybercrime laws.

Organization of cybercrime laws is also worth noting. Most states have chapters or subchapters in their codified laws dedicated to computer offenses. A handful of states, however, intersperse cybercrime provisions across various other criminal provisions. Ohio, for example, inserts computer crime provisions in several non-consecutive places within chapter 2909 of its codified laws, which is titled "Arson and Related Offenses."

The rest of this chapter summarizes some of the common components of cybercrime laws throughout the United States. Rather than discussing each state's cybercrime laws in their own section, this chapter will refer to recurring themes in general terms. Statutory sections are listed in an appendix. In lieu of individual state citations in this chapter, we have created tables listing several different aspects of state cybercrime laws and in which states those aspects are addressed. These tables are provided at the end of this chapter. If a state has a particular category of provision, its postal abbreviation is listed in the right column.

I.   SUBSTANTIVE LAW

States respond differently to changes in society, but it should come as no surprise that all fifty states emphasize the idea of authorization in their cybercrime laws. Whether something is authorized or exceeds authorized access is pivotal for the CFAA. The same is true in the states, though only twenty-five states explicitly prohibit actions that exceed authorized access.

Authorization is the subject of circuit splits under the CFAA. One of the fundamental questions at the federal level concerns how to tell whether an act counts as authorized, as the CFAA does not provide a definition for authorization. At the state level, twenty-one states define authorization in some form. Some states frame the definition as what it means to be without authorization, others from the view of what it means for someone to be an authorized user. Definitions range from tautological (*e.g.* an authorized user is a user who is authorized) to detailed definitions that reference implicit and explicit consent.

In the CFAA, there is a misdemeanor provision that is based solely on unauthorized access that results in obtaining information, while the felony provisions require unauthorized access *plus* something else—for example, unauthorized access *plus* the intent to commit a criminal or tortious offense. In the states, thirty-eight states have cybercrime laws that include a broad ban on unauthorized access, and almost all states consider intent or effects related to unauthorized access. The most common category of provisions concerns when unauthorized access is combined with actions that alter, damage, or destroy computers, networks, programs, or data. States often use multiple verbs to capture the ideas, but the central concept that a lot of states look for is change enabled by unauthorized access. Some laws are more specific. Twenty-eight states have laws against introducing computer contaminants without authorization, and fifteen states have laws against unauthorized spyware. In

April 2018, the Georgia legislature passed a bill expanding its cybercrime law to make mere unauthorized access a misdemeanor, with no adverse effects required. The governor vetoed the bill, citing the concern that the scope of the bill could hinder efforts to protect against cyberattacks.

Cybercrimes are also defined and differentiated based on intent. Thirty-six states have cybercrime laws that cover access for the purpose of obtaining things of value, thirty-eight include access for the purpose of committing fraud, and twenty-seven include access for the purpose of obtaining computer services. Ten states prohibit the use of a computer to commit a separate crime. In section 73.9 of Louisiana's cybercrime law, for instance, using a virtual street map to aid in the commission of a crime adds at least a year to the sentence for the underlying offense.

Cybercrime laws also frequently address actions on data that may not amount to a change in the system. Thirty-five states address actions that involve disclosing, using, controlling, or taking data without authority. Through provisions like this, cybercrime laws sometimes overlap with data breach laws, which are addressed in a later chapter. Sixteen states specifically prohibit obtaining information concerning a person through unauthorized means, and fifteen prohibit the taking of confidential information. Thirteen states specifically address distributing or using account access information like passwords and account numbers. Eight states make it an offense to receive data that was obtained unlawfully.

Some laws apply to specific tools that can be related to cybercrime. Thirty states prohibit actions designed to disrupt a system or cause a denial of service. As noted above, twenty-eight states prohibit the unauthorized introduction of computer contaminants, and fifteen states prohibit the unauthorized introduction of spyware. Computer contaminants are generally defined as including malicious software. Fourteen states have cybercrime laws that address keystroke logging software. Thirteen states prohibit the act of deceiving others into installing software. The latter are generally in the context of spyware prohibitions.

Twenty states address phishing and/or other unlawful acts involving email. Seven of those states prohibit distributing or trafficking in software that falsifies email transmission information, which is a tool that might be used in phishing campaigns or to disseminate spam. The state of Washington explicitly prohibits spoofing, which the law describes as the unauthorized and knowing transmission of someone else's identifying information for the purpose of gaining unauthorized access with the intent of committing a crime.

Some states that address cybercrime tools go even further by addressing the use of encryption, which is fundamental to secure communications on the Internet. Five states prohibit the use of encryption in the process of committing a criminal offense. One of these five states is Minnesota, which includes Section

609.8912, titled "Criminal use of encryption." In this section, Minnesota law also prohibits the intentional use of encryption "to prevent, impede, delay, or disrupt the normal operation or use of another's computer, computer program, or computer system." Alaska has perhaps the broadest encryption reference in their cybercrime law. Section 11.46.740(a)(1)(G) of Alaska's cybercrime law simply makes it a criminal offense for someone to knowingly "encrypt[ ] or decrypt[ ] data" if they have "no right to do so." Texas includes "unlawful decryption" in their penal code, and Section 33.024 makes unlawful decryption a criminal offense "if the person intentionally decrypts encrypted private information through deception and without a legitimate business purpose."

Some of the laws are clearly patchwork fixes to address specific problems that arose around the time of a particular legislative session. Michigan and Texas both have specific provisions aimed at Phantom-ware and similar devices that can be used to exploit vulnerabilities in point of sale systems. Louisiana, Mississippi, Texas, and Rhode Island have an offense called Online Impersonation, which we will revisit in the identity theft chapter. Texas amended its penal code in 2017 to specifically prohibit the use of ransomware under Section 33.023. Colorado has a law against the use of ticket line-skipping software, and Indiana's legislature adopted a slightly broader law with a similar target, which is described in the statute as merchandise-hoarding software. In both Colorado and Indiana, the goal seems to be to address the use of software to make purchases online in a manner that is unfair to customers who do not use an automated shopping tool. Nine states include cyber harassment laws within their cybercrime statutes. We did not analyze provisions within cybercrime chapters about computer-assisted offenses that were too far out of the realm of security and privacy, like solicitation of a minor and child pornography offenses. The most unique example within a chapter or subchapter of computer offenses was in Pennsylvania. Under 18 Pa. Cons. Stat. Ann. § 7641, livestock owners are prohibited from engaging in the computer-assisted remote harvesting of animals.

Only five states seem to acknowledge non-malicious hacking in their cybercrime statutes. Florida's law about offenses against computer users includes an exception for someone who "[p]erforms authorized security operations of a government or business." Nevada includes an exception for penetration testing, and Texas provides a defense based on conduct that was completed with the purpose of assessing security. Washington's law goes so far as to explicitly define "white hat security research" in its definition section. Utah arguably goes the furthest of the five by creating an affirmative defense based on conduct that is in response to a prior breach of security.

Some crimes can be characterized as upstream or downstream because they enable a separate criminal activity or they are enabled by a separate criminal activity. In the CFAA, the only upstream provision concerns trafficking in passwords and similar access

information. Some states criminalize upstream
crimes like trafficking in software that enables email
spoofing. By enacting such laws, states are looking
upstream to the provider of tools that enable someone
else to cause harm. Other states have cybercrime
laws that also look downstream to the recipient of
unlawfully obtained information, similar to the
federal Economic Espionage Act's prohibition on
receiving unlawfully obtained trade secrets. By
criminalizing the receipt of unlawfully obtained
information, legislators are looking downstream of
the data thief to the potentially more identifiable
information recipients.

II. PENALTIES

The punishment classes for various cybercrimes
vary between states. Alaska is the only state with a
cybercrime statute that only has one class of penalty
(Class C felony). All other states either vary their
punishments based on the specific provision violated
or based on the provision combined with other
factors. Eight states varied penalties or classes by
provision alone. The other 41 used other elements to
differentiate violations.

Nineteen states provided for different
punishments based on affected parties—for example,
if the target was a government agency or an
organization focused on public safety. Fifteen states
increase penalties for some provisions based on
effects on critical infrastructure. Thirty-nine states
vary penalties based on the level of monetary harm,
often in a range. For instance, monetary harm less

than $500 might be one punishment class, while monetary harm between $500 and $1500 is another. Twelve states consider non-monetary effects when assigning penalties, like if an action created a risk of physical injury. Sixteen states increase penalties for subsequent violations of the cybercrime law, and twenty states consider situational or motivational factors, like actions that were taken with the intent to defraud.

At the risk of making a distinction without a difference, it should be noted that some of the elements that increase penalties in some states show up in other states' laws as part of the substantive provisions. For example, some states address actions with the intent to defraud as part of the prohibition on behavior, while other states only address intent to defraud in the penalty subsection. In a state where intent to defraud enhances the penalty, acting with intent to defraud might turn a first degree misdemeanor into a third degree felony. Of course, this can also effectively be the case when the intent to defraud is addressed in the substantive definition of the offense.

In addition to the different factors that influence penalties, states often provide for other means of redress. Twelve states address forfeiture related to violations of cybercrime laws, and more may also address forfeiture in more general provisions in their state codes. Twenty-seven states give injured parties the ability to bring civil suits based on violations of the cybercrime laws. Most of the laws pertaining to phishing and spyware only include civil penalties.

III. RECENT CHANGES

As noted above, state cybercrime laws change frequently. This brief section is about the efforts of a single state, Washington, whose legislature adopted a new approach to cybercrime laws in 2016. The legislature's findings emphasize their collective belief that a new approach is needed for cybercrime—more than just a set of laws about old crimes committed in new ways. The Washington legislature's efforts use Microsoft's STRIDE cyber threat modeling system as a guide. STRIDE stands for:

- **S**poofing
- **T**ampering with data
- **R**epudiation
- **I**nformation disclosure
- **D**enial of service
- **E**levation of privilege

These six categories cover a range of activities. Spoofing involves the unauthorized use of another person's authentication information. Washington is not the only state to acknowledge the threat of spoofing, though most states that do so address it in the context of phishing laws that usually involve some other injury beyond the spoofed identity. Data Tampering refers to malicious modification. In computer security, repudiation refers to actions without accountability. Repudiation threats emerge when intruders are able to "hide their tracks." Such threats are largely addressed through industry best practices that emphasize logs and audit trails that track every action in a system. The Information disclosure threat category encompasses data breaches and other privacy threats that occur as a result of an intrusion, while the Denial of service threat category covers risks that impact service availability. An attacker who takes advantage of system weaknesses to Elevate their own privilege in the system can force fundamental changes throughout the system that only the most trusted administrators should be able to make.

The revisions made to Washington cybercrime law are still very new. The changes mostly represent a teleological shift for how to visualize the risks that cybercrime laws are intended to address. Whether the STRIDE threat model is an optimal approach for legislation remains to be seen. The Washington legislature's approach at least indicates an expanding notion of cyber harms, and these are exactly the kinds of changes that practitioners should be prepared to address.

State Tables: Access and Authorization

Provision	States							
Access + altering, damaging, or destroying programs or data	AL	AK	AZ	AR	CA	CO	CT	DE
	FL	GA	HI	ID	IL		IA	KS
		LA	ME	MD		MI	MN	MS
	MO	MT	NE	NV	NH	NJ	NM	NY
	NC	ND	OH		OR	PA	RI	SC
	SD	TN	TX	UT	VT	VA	WA	WV
	WI	WY						
Access + altering, damaging, or destroying computers/ networks	AL	AK	AZ	AR	CA	CO	CT	DE
	FL	GA	HI	ID	IL	IN		KS
	KY	LA	ME	MD		MI	MN	MS
	MO	MT	NE	NV	NH	NJ	NM	
	NC	ND	OH	OK	OR	PA	RI	SC
	SD	TN	TX	UT	VT	VA		WV
	WI	WY						
Access for the purpose of committing fraud				AR		CO		
	FL	GA	HI	ID	IL	IN		KS
	KY	LA			MA	MI	MN	MS
	MO	MT	NE	NV		NJ	NM	
	NC	ND	OH	OK	OR	PA	RI	SC
		TN	TX	UT	VT	VA	WA	WV
	WI	WY						

						CO		
	FL	GA	HI	ID	IL	IN		KS
	KY	LA				MI	MN	MS
Access for the purpose of obtaining things of value	MO	MT	NE	NV		NJ	NM	
	NC	ND	OH	OK	OR	PA	RI	SC
	SD	TN		UT	VT	VA	WA	WV
	WI	WY						
			AZ		CA	CO	CT	DE
	FL		HI		IL	IN	IA	KS
	KY	LA	ME	MD	MA		MN	
	MO		NE	NV	NH	NJ	NM	NY
Broad ban on unauthorized access	NC	ND	OH	OK	OR	PA		
	SD	TN	TX	UT	VT		WA	
	WI	WY						
				AR	CA	CO	CT	
		GA	HI					
			ME				MN	
					NH	NJ		NY
Defining authorization or authorized user	NC					PA	RI	SC
		TN		UT		VA	WA	WV
	AL	AK	AZ			CO	CT	
		GA	HI		IL			KS
		LA	ME	MD		MI		
Exceeding authorization			NE			NJ	NM	
	NC	ND	OH	OK		PA	RI	

	SD			UT		VA		
					CA		CT	DE
					IL			
				MD	MA	MI	MN	MS
		MT	NE	NV	NH	NJ	NM	
Access to obtain computer services	NC		OH	OK		PA	RI	SC
	SD	TN		UT	VT	VA		WV

State Tables: Data Offenses

Provision	States							
Disclosing, using, controlling, or taking data	AL						CT	DE
	FL	GA	HI	ID	IL		IA	KS
		LA	ME	MD		MI	MN	MS
	MO		NE	NV	NH	NJ		NY
	NC	ND	OH			PA	RI	SC
	SD		TX	UT	VT	VA	WA	
	WI	WY						
Obtains confidential information	AL	AK	AZ					
	FL		HI				IA	
		LA					MN	MS
			NE			NJ		
					OR			
	SD							WV
		WY						
Obtains any data					CA		CT	
			HI		IL		IA	KS
		LA		MD			MN	
			NE			NJ		NY
	NC	ND				PA		
	SD							WV

		AK	AZ	AR	CA			
		GA					IA	
		LA					MN	
	MO					NJ		
Obtains information concerning a person						PA	RI	
			TX	UT		VA		WV
							CT	DE
	KY							
	MO			NH				NY
Receives data obtained unlawfully		TN						WV

State Tables: Tools and Methods

Provision	States							
Disrupting system or causing denial of service	AL		AZ	AR	CA		CT	DE
	FL	GA				IN		
		LA					MN	MS
	MO		NE	NV	NH	NJ	NM	
	NC	ND		OK		PA		SC
	SD		TX	UT	VT		WA	WV
	WI	WY						
Prohibition on key stroke loggers		AK	AZ	AR	CA			
		GA					IA	
		LA						
					NH			
						PA	RI	
			TX	UT		VA	WA	
Use of encryption related to committing a criminal offense				AR				
					IL			
							MN	
				NV				
						VA		
Introducing computer contaminants	AL		AZ	AR	CA	CO		
	FL	GA			IL	IN	IA	
		LA	ME			MI	MN	MS

		NE	NV	NH	NJ		
NC	ND	OH			PA		
	TN	TX				WA	WV
	WY						
	LA						
				NH			
		TX				WA	
Botnets							

State Tables: Other Offenses

Provision	States								
							CT		
					IL				
		LA							
Trafficking in software that falsifies email transmission information				NV					
						PA	RI		
						VA			
				AR	CA		CT	DE	
					IL				
		LA		MD					
				NV					
Unlawful acts involving email	NC					PA	RI		
		TN	TX			VA			
	AL			AR	CA		CT		
					IL				
	KY	LA							
		MT							NY
				OK			RI		
Phishing		TN	TX	UT					
		AK	AZ	AR	CA				
		GA			IL	IN	IA		
Spyware		LA							

				NH				
					PA	RI		
		TX	UT			WA		
Using a computer to commit a separate crime								
		HI						
	LA				MI			
							NY	
		OH	OK			RI	SC	
					VA	WA		
Using a computer to terrorize or harass another person		AZ	AR					
NC			OK			RI		
			UT		VA		WV	
WI								
Deceiving others into installing software		AZ	AR	CA				
	GA				IN	IA		
	LA							
				NH				
					PA	RI		
		TX	UT			WA		

State Tables: Punishment

Provision	States							
Punishment factors: Critical infrastructure targeted	AL		AZ					
	FL		HI		IL	IN	IA	
		LA		MD				
				NV		NJ		
			OH					
			TX					WV
		WY						
Punishment factors: Monetary harm	AL			AR	CA	CO	CT	DE
	FL		HI		IL	IN	IA	KS
	KY	LA		MD		MI	MN	MS
	MO	MT	NE	NV	NH	NJ	NM	NY
	NC		OH			PA	RI	SC
		TN	TX	UT	VT	VA		WV
	WI	WY						
Punishment factors: Non-monetary harm	AL							DE
	FL				IL	IN		
							MN	
			NE	NV	NH	NJ		
			OH					
	WI							
Punishment factors:				AR	CA	CO		
					IL			
						MI	MN	MS

Subsequent violations			NE		NH			NY
							RI	SC
			TX	UT	VT	VA		
			AZ					
							IA	
							MN	
Punishment factors: Type of data taken						NJ		NY
				UT		VA		
	AL		AZ				CT	
	FL		HI		IL	IN	IA	
		LA						
Punishment factors: Affected party			NE	NV		NJ		
	NC		OH		OR			
			TX			VA		WV
		WY						
				AR	CA	CO		
					IL			
						MI	MN	MS
Punishment factors: Situational or motivational			NE		NH			NY
							RI	SC
			TX	UT	VT	VA		

State Tables: Procedural Elements

Provision	States							
	AL		AZ	AR	CA	CO	CT	DE
		GA	HI					
	KY		ME	MD				MS
					NH	NJ		
	NC			OK		PA		SC
Addresses jurisdiction or venue	SD	TN	TX		VT	VA		WV
			AZ	AR	CA		CT	DE
	FL	GA			IL	IN	IA	
		LA						
	MO			NV		NJ		
	NC			OK		PA	RI	SC
		TN	TX	UT	VT	VA		WV
Civil remedy	WI	WY						
	AL		AZ		CA			
	FL		HI		IL			
			ME			MI		
					NH		NM	
					OR			
Forfeiture	WI							

CHAPTER 6
DATA BREACHES

At the time of this writing, there are no general federal data breach laws. While some federal legislation has been proposed, and some sector-specific federal information privacy statutes include requirements to follow in the event of a breach, today's data breach statutes are state laws. The adoption of state data breach laws was spread out over more than a decade. As of 2018, all fifty states have a data breach statute.

Data breach laws often specify what information needs to be protected under the law, when a breached company must provide notification and to whom, and whether civil actions may be brought by those whose data was breached. State data breach laws typically also address encryption. For example, the theft of encrypted data without the decryption key often will not trigger notification requirements under state data breach laws.

I. WHAT INFORMATION MUST BE PROTECTED UNDER THE LAW

Currently, all fifty states, the District of Columbia, Puerto Rico, Guam, and the Virgin Islands have laws regarding data breaches in effect. Alabama was the last state to adopt a data breach law, and it did so in April 2018. Most data breach laws follow a basic definition of what constitutes a breach of security and personal information that must be protected with minor variations. A breach of security is commonly defined as including the unauthorized acquisition of protected information that compromises that information's security, confidentiality, or integrity. Some states include unauthorized access in the definition of a breach. A minority of states diverge from the "security, confidentiality, or integrity" language in defining security breaches.

There are several shared traits in almost all state data breach laws. They all define categories of information that must be protected. Generally, "personal information" requires a name (the full last name and at least a first initial) combined with at least one other type of information. New York's law, though, does not require a name to be attached to the information as long as there is a combination of information affected.[1] Most states refer to encryption in their data breach laws, often in the context of defining what kind of loss of information constitutes a breach. Data breach laws typically apply to unencrypted data, but encrypted data may also be covered by a data breach law when the encryption key was also compromised.

For a majority of states, there are at least three types of information that are considered protected: 1) social security numbers, 2) driver's license numbers or the numbers from another government-issued identification card, and 3) financial account numbers (including credit and debit accounts) in combination with the verification information needed to access the account. Most states exclude information that is

---

[1]   N.Y. Gen. Bus. Law § 899–aa(1)(a).

lawfully found in publicly available sources, though many of them limit this category to government records. In addition to the big three (social security numbers, driver's licenses, financial accounts), many states include additional data categories as protected personal information. The District of Columbia, for example, includes an individual's phone number and address in its definition of personal information.

The most common additional protection is the protection of medical information, offered by fifteen states and Puerto Rico. These state laws cover a varying amount of information. For example, in Arkansas, medical information "means any individually identifiable information, in electronic or physical form, regarding the individual's medical history or medical treatment or diagnosis by a health care professional."[2] In Missouri, it means "any information regarding an individual's medical history, mental or physical condition, or medical treatment or diagnosis by a health care professional."[3] Texas uses a narrower definition that applies to information about "the physical or mental health or condition of the individual."[4] Texas also considers medical information to be "sensitive personal information" when the information relates to "the provision of health care to the individual" or payment for said health care.

---

[2]   Ark. Code § 4–110–101.

[3]   Mo. Rev. Stat. § 407.1500.

[4]   Tex. Bus. & Com. Code § 521.002.

Of the states that protect medical information, five of them—Alabama, California, Missouri, Nevada, and Texas—protect health insurance information. The protection in Nevada covers "a health insurance identification number." Missouri, alongside its definition for medical information above, defines health insurance information as "an individual's health insurance policy number or subscriber identification number, [or] any unique identifier used by a health insurer to identify the individual."[5]

Some states list other sources of identification information that are protected. Nine states provide for protection of a username or email in combination with a password or the answers to security questions.[6]

Biometric data is also an increasingly popular additional protection. Connecticut, Illinois, Iowa, Nebraska, New Mexico, North Carolina, Oregon, South Dakota, Wisconsin, and Wyoming include biometric data in their definitions for personal information. Wisconsin goes beyond the other states by also including an individual's DNA profile.[7] Three states—Georgia, Maine, and Oregon all protect any data sufficient for identity theft in general. New Jersey also includes "[d]issociated data that, if linked, would constitute personal information is personal information if the means to link the

---

[5]   Mo. Rev. Stat. § 407.1500.

[6]   *E.g.,* AL, FL, RI, SD, WY.

[7]   Wis. Stat. § 134.98(1)(b)(4).

dissociated data were accessed in connection with access to the dissociated data."[8]

Taxpayer identification numbers are specifically protected in Connecticut, Maryland, and Wyoming. Puerto Rico makes a provision for tax information. Information through license plate registration is protected in California. Connecticut protects alien registration numbers, Florida protects military identification numbers, and both protect passport numbers. Nebraska also includes "[u]nique electronic identification number or routing code, in combination with any required security code, access code, or password."[9]

North Dakota defines personal information to include several additional information types, including date of birth, the "maiden name of the individual's mother," and "identification number assigned to the individual by the individual's employer in combination with any required security code, access code, or password," and electronic signatures.[10] South Carolina protects the broad category of "other numbers or information which may be used to access a person's financial accounts or numbers or information issued by a governmental or regulatory entity that uniquely will identify an individual."[11] Wyoming protects birth or marriage

---

[8]   N.J. Stat. § 56:8–16.1.

[9]   Neb. Rev. Stat. § 87–802(5)(a)(iv).

[10]   N.D. Cent. Code § 51–30–01.

[11]   S.C. Code § 39–1–90(D)(3)(d).

certificates.[12] Finally, Puerto Rico protects work evaluations.[13]

II. WHEN MUST BREACHED ENTITIES PROVIDE NOTIFICATION AND TO WHOM

After a breach has been ascertained, states differ on who must receive notices. Common parties are the person whose information was stolen, the attorney general of the state, consumer reporting agencies, and other governmental entities. States have generally the same definition of what constitutes a breach, whether it be the "unauthorized acquisition . . . of personal information that compromises the security, confidentiality, or integrity of the personal information . . . ."[14] in Alaska or the "unauthorized acquisition of unencrypted and unredacted computerized data that compromises the security, confidentiality, or integrity of personally identifiable information"[15] in Kentucky.

There are other common aspects of state data breach laws. A majority of state data breach laws also apply to government agencies. Most state data breach laws also create exclusions for what is considered a breach. In Kentucky, "[g]ood-faith acquisition of personally identifiable information by an employee or agent of the information holder for the purposes of the information holder is not a breach

---

[12]   Wyo. Stat. § 40–12–501.
[13]   10 Laws of Puerto Rico § 4051.
[14]   Alaska Stat. § 45.48.010(1).
[15]   KRS § 365.732(1)(a).

of the security"[16] as long as that information is not itself used to help someone else breach the system. States also generally include provisions stating that any notification may be delayed so that it does not affect an investigation by a law enforcement agency.[17] Some have an additional provision that allows for delay in notification if it were to "jeopardize homeland or national security."[18] State laws also specify how notification should be conducted, usually through the mail or electronic notification.[19] Some states also allow notification by telephone, or by publishing in newspapers with broad circulation.[20]

States disagree on when a company must actually provide notice. Eighteen states[21] fall into the most popular category, under which if there is no reasonable likelihood of harm to the consumer, no notification needs to be made. As stated in Iowa's Personal Information Security Breach Protection, no notification is required if "no reasonable likelihood of financial harm to the consumers whose personal information has been acquired has resulted or will

---

[16]   *Id.*

[17]   *See e.g.*, KRS § 365.732(4); N.H. Rev. Stat. § 359–C:20(II); Utah Code § 13–44–202(4)(a), among others.

[18]   *See e.g.*, Md. Code Com. Law § 14–3504(d)(1)(i).

[19]   *See e.g.*, Ark. Code § 4–110–105(e); Fla. Stat. § 501.171(4)(d).

[20]   *See e.g.*, Utah Code § 13–44–202(5); Ohio Rev. Code § 1347.12(E).

[21]   AL, AK, AR, CT, HA, IA, KS, KY, LA, ME, NH, NJ, NC, OR, SC, UT, VT, WA.

result from the breach."[22] The ordinary way to determine whether there is a likelihood of harm is whether the breached data was encrypted or redacted.[23]

States use different wordings to describe when the statute's notification requirements will be triggered. South Carolina qualifies its definition of a breach by limiting it to "when the illegal use of the information has occurred or is reasonably likely to occur or use of the information creates a material risk of harm to the resident."[24] Neither Ohio nor Wisconsin requires notice when the illegal acquisition does not create a "material risk of identity theft."[25] In Massachusetts, the breach must create a "substantial risk of identity theft or fraud" before notice is required.[26] In Rhode Island, notification is not required unless there is "a significant risk of identity theft." In Maryland, notification is only required once the data holder's investigation has concluded "that misuse of the individual's personal information has occurred or is reasonably likely to occur."[27] Whether notification is required thus often relies on the data protector's judgment of when a risk is reasonably likely, significant, material, or substantial.

---

[22]   Iowa Code § 715C.2(6).

[23]   S.C. Code § 39–1–90(A).

[24]   *Id.*

[25]   Ohio   Rev.   Code   § 1347.12(B)(1);   Wis.   Stat. § 134.98(2)(cm)(1).

[26]   Mass. Gen. Laws § 93H(a).

[27]   Md. Code Com. Law § 14–3504(b)(2).

Nine states and the District of Columbia require notice to anyone whose personal information was reasonably believed to have been acquired during the breach.[28] The general language used in these statutes is simple. For example, in North Dakota notification must be made to any resident "whose unencrypted personal information was, or is reasonably believed to have been, acquired by an unauthorized person."[29] Texas uses slightly different language, providing for only "sensitive personal information."[30]

Eight states require an investigation to determine whether or not misuse of personal information is likely to occur, and if not, then no notification is required.[31] In Idaho, any entity which has been breached must "conduct in good faith a reasonable and prompt investigation to determine the likelihood that personal information has been or will be misused," and only "[i]f the investigation determines that the misuse of information about an Idaho resident has occurred or is reasonably likely to occur, the agency, individual or the commercial entity shall give notice . . . ."[32] Mississippi uses negative language to describe obligations, saying that "[n]otification shall not be required if, after an appropriate investigation, the person reasonably

---

[28]   CA, GA, IL, IN, MN, NY, ND, OK, TX.

[29]   N.D. Cent. Code, § 51–30–02.

[30]   Tex. Bus. & Com. Code § 521.053(c).

[31]   CO, DE, FL, ID, MI, MS, MO, NE.

[32]   Idaho Code § 28–51–105.

determines that the breach will not likely result in harm to the affected individuals."[33]

Seven states do not require notification if the breach does not materially compromise the security of personal information.[34] All require immediate notification, but define breach in such a way that it is only triggered in this circumstance. For example, Arizona requires notification "in the most expedient manner possible and without unreasonable delay" if an investigation determines there has been a breach, but defines breach so that it triggers only when the breach "materially compromises the security or confidentiality of personal information[,]"[35] a finding that requires some form of investigation first. Nevada has a similar statute, requiring notification to any resident whose information was reasonably believed to have been acquired,[36] but defines a breach as an "unauthorized acquisition of computerized data that materially compromises the security, confidentiality or integrity of personal information . . . ."[37]

Virginia and West Virginia also have high bars for notification. In Virginia, a breach only encompasses situations which the entity "reasonably believes has caused, or will cause, identity theft or other fraud."[38]

---

[33]   Miss. Code § 75–24–29.

[34]   AZ, MT, NV, PA, SD, TN, WY.

[35]   A.R.S. § 18–545.

[36]   Nev. Rev. Stat. Ann. § 603A.220(1).

[37]   Nev. Rev. Stat. Ann. § 603A.020.

[38]   Va. Code Ann. § 18.2–186.6(A).

West Virginia's wording is very similar.[39] Most other states that use similar language base the reporting requirement on risk. In New Mexico, if the data breach "does not give rise to a significant risk of identity theft or fraud," no notification is required.[40]

States also vary on when the state attorney general needs to be notified of the breach. Alaska and Connecticut entities must notify their attorneys general if there is a reasonable likelihood of harm. In Illinois, North Dakota, Oregon, and South Dakota, this notification requirement is triggered when 250 residents are affected. In five other states,[41] 500 residents must be affected, while in Alabama, Missouri, and New Mexico, 1000 residents must be affected before the notification requirement is triggered. In Idaho, if is the victim is a public agency, the attorney general must be notified regardless of the number affected. In some states the AG must be notified as soon as the breach is discovered.[42] Maryland requires that the attorney general be notified prior to any state residents.[43]

Most states require breached entities to notify consumer reporting agencies (CRAs) on the breach at a certain threshold. Minnesota and Rhode Island require that if 500 residents must be notified, then CRAs must also be informed. Twenty-seven states

---

[39] W. Va. Code § 46A–2A–101(1).

[40] N.M. Stat. § 57–12C–6.

[41] CA, FL, IA, RI, WA.

[42] ID, IN, ME, MD, MA, NE, NY, VT, VA.

[43] Md. Code Com. Law §§ 14–3504(h).

and DC put this threshold at 1,000 residents.[44] New York puts its threshold at 5,000 residents, while Georgia and Texas put theirs at 10,000 residents. Iowa does not require direct notification of CRAs, but it does require notification to residents to include contact information for CRAs. Similarly, Massachusetts does not require direct notification by the breached entity, but the Director of Consumer Affairs and Business Regulation will automatically notify CRAs for a breach of any size.

Many states also require notice be sent to government agencies other than the Attorney General's office. Montana requires notice be sent to the state's Central Information Officer at the Department of Administration, which is also something Idaho requires but only if the breached entity is a state agency. Hawaii requires notice to the Office of Consumer Reporting. Massachusetts requires that the Director of Consumer Affairs and Business Regulation be notified. In Maine, entities must notify the Department of Professional and Financial Regulation if they are regulated by it, and if not then directly to the attorney general. In New Jersey, prior to any other notification, the Division of State Policy in the Department of Law & Public Safety must be notified. In New York, the Department of State and the Division of State Police must be notified. Finally, in South Carolina if 1,000 residents are affected by the breach, the Consumer

---

[44]   AL, AK, CO, FL, HI, IN, KS, KY, ME, MD, MI, MO, NV, NH, NJ, NM, NC, OH, OR, PA, SC, TEN, VT, VA, WV, WI.

Protection Division of the Department of Consumer Affairs must be notified.

In three states, additional notice requirements apply to breaches that affect medical information. California and Washington both require notice to health services if medical information is breached. In Virginia, the attorney general must be notified if medical information is breached.

III. PRIVATE CAUSE OF ACTION

Thirteen states allow residents to file civil actions against the breached entities, as well as DC, Puerto Rico, and the Virgin Islands.[45] In many statutes, the cause of action is based on state unfair trade practice laws.[46] Louisiana allows civil actions to recover actual damages caused by the breach. Massachusetts allows up to treble damages. North Carolina has a maximum of $5,000 plus treble damages. Injunctive relief is also available in three of these states— California, North Carolina, and South Carolina. Oregon allows for private civil actions, but also allows for compensation to be ordered if civil actions are impractical.

There is some variety in laws that recognize causes of action associated with data breaches. In Nevada, no private cause of action is available for the consumer, but the data collector may bring suit against the person(s) who breached the system. Some

---

[45]   AK, CA, LA, MD, MA, NH, NC, OR, SC, SD, TN, TX, VA, WA.

[46]   *See, e.g.*, Alaska Stat. § 45.50.470.

states create a right of action for certain categories of breached data. New Hampshire allows for civil actions against the data collector when a breach affects medical information.

IV. ENCRYPTION REQUIRED

States also generally address encryption's role in whether a breach triggers the statute. There are some states where notification is required for the loss of encrypted data if the means of decrypting is also lost. Otherwise, data breach statutes generally apply only to data that is unencrypted. For example, in Missouri the statute only applies "if any of the data elements are not encrypted, redacted, or otherwise altered by any method or technology in such a manner that the name or data elements are unreadable or unusable."[47] Missouri defines encryption as "an algorithmic process to transform data into a form in which the data is rendered unreadable or unusable without the use of a confidential process or key."[48] The states in this category all follow the general rule of defining encryption as a transformation of data so it cannot be used "without use of a confidential process or key."[49] If the key is also lost in the breach, the notification requirement will often activate.

---

[47] Mo. Rev. Stat. § 407.1500(1)(9).

[48] Mo. Rev. Stat. § 407.1500(1)(4).

[49] Ohio Rev. Code § 1347.12(A)(4).

V. LITIGATING DATA BREACHES

While some state data breach laws create a cause of action, a lot of the litigation brought in the aftermath of data breaches draws on common law. One distinction that might increasingly become important is the distinction between data breaches and data misuse, though at the moment, courts frequently do not make the distinction.

Whenever a data breach occurs, the common factor is a loss of exclusivity for the breached information. A data breach might lead to a variety of outcomes, but the breach exists because information that was supposed to have a limited audience was exposed outside of that audience. Data misuse, on the other hand, exists when there is an unauthorized data use. Identity theft is not directly caused by a data breach, but rather by a misuse of sensitive data. Data breaches and data misuses thus may occur together or separately. While a data breach might be accidental, data misuse would generally involve a volitional act by someone.

While it would be more desirable to hold wrong-doers accountable, that is very difficult in the context of data breaches, and so the focus in data breach lawsuits has generally been the first level victim of the breach—that is, the entity whose computer systems were compromised. In his book, The Cost of Accidents, Guido Calabresi argues that civil litigation can be used to control the costs of accidents and shift the burden to the party best able to prevent the accident. Under this view, data breach liability for first level victims is important for the overall goal of increasing security. By increasing the incentives to secure data, either through carrots or sticks, government actions can contribute to a stronger cybersecurity environment.

In the United States, data breach lawsuits are far from predictable. An empirical study found that breached entities are more likely to be sued when the breach affected more people or when individuals have already suffered financial harm from the breach.[50] Entities that provided free credit monitoring to victims have historically been sued at lower rates.[51] Offering free credit monitoring does not seem to have a significant downside in litigation, and courts have generally rejected arguments that offering free credit monitoring is an admission of guilt.[52]

In Romanosky's data set, 76% of the lawsuits were class actions. Once a data breach lawsuit is brought, Romanosky's calculations suggest that there is approximately a 50/50 chance that the lawsuit will end in a settlement. Many of the remaining lawsuits still do not make it out of the pretrial stage. The same study found no fewer than 86 unique causes of action in data breach cases. Some of the common claims were founded in state unfair business practice laws, the federal Fair Credit Reporting Act, breach of contract, and negligence.

---

[50]　Sasha Romanosky, David Hoffman & Alessandro Acquisti, *Empirical Analysis of Data Breach Litigation*, 11 J. EMPIRICAL LEGAL STUDIES 74, 74 (March 2014).

[51]　*Id.*

[52]　*E.g.*, Beck v. McDonald, 848 F.3d 262, 276 (4th Cir. 2017).

Injuries caused by data privacy violations are difficult to quantify, and this causes a problem for data breach litigation. Many data breach lawsuits that are filed in federal court do not even reach the merits stage because they are dismissed as lacking the concrete and particularized injury required for Article 3 standing. Dismissals for lack of standing in federal cases are often based on case law concerning standing for future injuries.

In 2013, the Supreme Court decided Clapper v. Amnesty International.[53] The case concerned whether Amnesty International had standing to challenge the constitutionality of warrantless surveillance. In a 5–4 decision, the Court held that the possible future harm of warrantless surveillance was too speculative for the injury to be "certainly impending." Amnesty International had made costly changes to protect their communications against surveillance, but the Court rejected that theory of injury as well, stating that "respondents cannot manufacture standing by choosing to make expenditures based on hypothetical future harm that is not certainly impending."

In data breach cases without fraud already alleged, standing analysis thus often focuses on whether harm is certainly impending. Generally, the harm that the courts look for is financial harm. Even in cases where individuals experience credit card fraud, the card issuers typically absorb the loss, so the person who is at risk of identity theft might not

---

[53]   Clapper v. Amnesty Int'l, 568 U.S. 398 (2013).

have standing to sue. Identity theft can be costly to fix, but plaintiffs who have not yet suffered identity theft have not taken on those costs. Most individual victims will have paid, at most, for credit monitoring and other minor transactional costs. Some plaintiffs have compared their injuries to medical monitoring cases where the injury is largely tied to the anxiety of developing a disease in the future.

Beck v. McDonald is a Fourth Circuit data breach standing case brought after the theft of four boxes of pathology reports and a laptop containing unencrypted patient files. The court did not find a substantial risk of identity theft harm, so they rejected the argument that the theft was enough for standing. One of the reasons that the court did not find standing was that such a finding would require too many assumptions, like that the laptop was stolen for the information contained within it.

While some courts have used *Clapper* when dismissing data breach claims for lack of standing, there are other courts that have ruled the other way. In Galaria v. Nationwide Mutual Insurance Company, the Sixth Circuit found that data breach plaintiffs had alleged a substantial risk of future harm sufficient for standing.[54] The Seventh Circuit has likewise found in two cases that data breaches can cause injuries for the purposes of standing.[55] Like *Galaria*, in *Remijas*, the Seventh Circuit concluded

---

[54]   663 F. App'x. 384, 388 (6th Cir. 2016).

[55]   Remijas v. Neiman Marcus Group, LLC, 794 F.3d 688 (7th Cir. 2015); Lewert v. P.F. Chang's China Bistro, Inc., 819 F.3d 963 (7th Cir. 2016).

that there was a substantial risk of future harm.[56] The Eighth Circuit in *In re Supervalu*, on the other hand, did not find substantial risk of future identity theft harms, but still found that data breach plaintiffs had standing based on a present injury.[57] This was because one of the people whose credit card information was breached experienced a fraudulent charge on the card after the breach.

Data breach lawsuits often involve financial information or other confidential personal information. In *Galaria*, the breached defendant was an insurance company, and the compromised information included names, birthdates, social security numbers, and driver's license numbers. *Remijas, Lewert,* and *In re Supervalu* concerned the theft of payment card information.

Shortly after *Clapper*, the Supreme Court revisited standing in Spokeo v. Robins. *Spokeo* was about standing based on the defendant's violation of the FCRA. In *Spokeo*, the plaintiff sued a personal data aggregating company for displaying false information about him. The Court concluded that there was no harm alleged in this false posting.[58]

In 2017, the Third Circuit applied *Spokeo* to a data breach case and found harm sufficient for standing.[59]

---

[56]   *Remijas*, 794 F.3d at 693.

[57]   Alleruzzo v. SuperValu, Inc. (In re SuperValu, Inc., Customer Data Sec. Breach Litig.), 870 F.3d 763, 774 (8th Cir. 2017).

[58]   Spokeo, Inc. v. Robins, 136 S. Ct. 1540, 1550 (2016).

[59]   In re Horizon Healthcare Servs. Inc. Data Breach Litig., 846 F.3d 625, 636 (3d Cir. 2017).

The *Horizon* litigation was based on the FCRA, just like the *Spokeo* litigation, but the Third Circuit based its decision on precedent that economic loss is not the proper measure of harm for standing purposes when standing is based on a violation of a privacy law. The Third Circuit thus implicitly concluded that the *Spokeo* plaintiff had not experienced any kind of loss from the posting of false information, economic or otherwise. Those affected by the *Horizon* data breach, on the other hand, had their privacy violated because true information was disseminated.

CHAPTER 7

IDENTITY THEFT—FEDERAL

Identity theft laws in the United States have wide variation across all fifty states and at the federal level. We will start with an overview of the federal law currently in place and then proceed to cover state laws and the commonalities and differences between them.

The federal law in place for the United States (18 U.S.C. § 1028) covers eight different scenarios, using various requisite intents and acts. All of these crimes are classified as "fraud and related activity in connection with identification documents." The first, section 1028(a)(1), prohibits knowingly producing an identification document. The second punishes transferring identification documents knowing they are stolen or made unlawfully. Third, it is a crime to possess with the intent to unlawfully use or transfer five or more identification documents (other than one's own documents or with the permission of the owner). Fourth, under section 1028(a)(4), it is a crime to knowingly possess an identification document (with the same exceptions as above) to defraud the United States.

The fifth violation, section 1028(a)(5), does not necessarily fall into the same category as the other seven listed in the federal law. It covers when one has, transfers, or makes a "document-making implement or authentication feature" with the intent it will be used to make a false document or another document-making implement.

Section 1028(a)(6) prohibits possession of an identification document or authentication feature of the United States knowing it was stolen or unlawfully produced. The seventh is knowingly transferring, possessing, or using a means of identification belonging to another person with the intent to commit any federal offense or a felony of any state. Finally, one cannot knowingly traffic in false or actual authentication features to use on false identification documents under section 1028(a)(8). The statute defines authentication features to include things like watermarks.

The federal identity theft statute has five verbs associated with the offenses: produce, transfer, possess, use, and traffic. Most of the violations contained in Section 1028(a) require something more than mere possession. Section 1028(a)(3) prohibits possession of five or more identification documents with the intent to use or transfer the documents unlawfully. Section 1028(a)(4) prohibits possession with the intent to defraud the United States. Section 1028(a)(5) prohibits possessing document-making tools or authentication feature with the intent that these items contribute to the production of false identification documents. Section 1028(a)(7) prohibits possessing identification documents belonging to another person with the intent to commit a crime. The exception to this is Section 1028(a)(6), which prohibits the possession of identification documents issued by the federal government when the possessor knows that the document was stolen or produced without lawful authority.

In the federal identity theft statute, like most state identity theft laws, there are varying degrees of punishment depending on the circumstances of the crime. The maximum sentence for most offenses is fifteen years when the forged identification document is a birth certificate or a government-issued identification or when the charge involves "the production or transfer of more than five identification documents . . ." Violations of 1028(a)(5) are also punishable with a maximum of fifteen years. Violations of 1028(a)(7) are punishable with a maximum of fifteen years if the defendant obtained $1,000 or more in value from the violation, and a maximum of five years if the defendant's benefit was valued at less than $1,000. The maximum sentence is five years for a violation of 1028(a)(3).

The punishment may be increased to a maximum of twenty years if any violation is committed while facilitating drug trafficking, in connection with a crime of violence, or after a prior conviction. It may be a maximum of thirty years where the violation facilitates an act of domestic or international terrorism. Attempt and conspiracy to commit these violations have the same penalties as the actual offenses. Violations of the mere possession provision, Section 1028(a)(6), are punishable by up to a year in prison if it is not accompanied by any of the other aggravating factors listed in Section 1028(b).

The identification documents used in this section are generally any government-issued identifying documents, including birth certificates, driver's licenses, or personal identification cards.

Additionally, the section defines "means of identification," which has a lot of overlap with the concept of "personally identifiable information." The federal identity theft law includes the following under what it considers to be a means of identification: name; social security number; date of birth; driver's license; alien registration number; government passport; employer or taxpayer identification number; biometric data (including fingerprint, voice print, retina image, iris image, or other unique physical characteristics); electronic identification numbers, addresses, or routing codes; or telecommunication identifying information or access devices. All of those and more are included in various combinations in state identity theft laws as well.

The United States also has another federal statute (18 U.S.C. § 1028A) that covers aggravated identity theft. There are only two varieties of this offense. The first is knowingly using, possessing, or transferring the means of identification of another in connection with one of the felonies enumerated in Section 1028A(c). A violation of this adds two years to whatever punishment the underlying felony gives. The second is knowingly trafficking in false or actual authentication features in connection with terrorism. The punishment for this is an additional five years to the sentence for the underlying felony offense.

The underlying offenses that support prosecution for aggravated identity theft are all federal crimes, and several of these crimes relate to immigration. Section 1028A(c)(2) refers to 18 U.S.C. § 911, which prohibits falsely presenting oneself as a United States citizen. Section 1028A(c)(6) and 1028A(c)(7) make it aggravated identity theft when the theft is associated with any felony violation of Chapters 69 and 75 in Title 18 of the United States code. Chapter 69 pertains to nationality and citizenship, and Chapter 75 pertains to passports and visas. Certain violations of the Immigration and Nationality Act are also predicate acts for aggravated identity theft. Other offenses that elevate identity theft to aggravated identity theft include categories of fraud and financial crimes.

Through the aggravated identity theft provision, federal identity theft law reinforces federal immigration law, but this reinforcement is not unlimited. In 2009, the Supreme Court issued a unanimous decision in Flores-Figueroa v. United States.[1] Ignacio Flores-Figueroa was an undocumented immigrant from Mexico. In 2000, he used a fake resident alien card and social security number in the name of Horatio Ramirez to obtain employment with a steel company. In 2006, Flores-Figueroa purchased forged identification documents with his own name. While the Ramirez identification documents had pertained to a fictional identity and no real person possessed the Ramirez social security number, the new identification documents included a social security number associated with an actual person. Flores-Figueroa was charged with violating 18 U.S.C. § 1546 (misuse of immigration documents), a felony included in Chapter 75 of Title 18, and thus

---

[1]   556 U.S. 646 (2009).

a predicate offense for the purpose of charging him with aggravated identity theft.

The federal identity statute, though, requires a particular mental state. All of the violations of Section 1028 and Section 1028A require actions to be taken knowingly. Flores-Figueroa, it was argued, knew that he had been sold forged documents, but he did not know that he had been sold a real social security number. The government argued that the knowledge requirement did not extend to whether the defendant knew that the identification information belonged to another person. The Supreme Court disagreed with the government's attorneys, and reversed the Eighth Circuit's decision.

After *Flores-Figueroa*, the federal identity theft statute should be read as requiring the perpetrator to have knowledge that another person's identification information was being used if the violated provision refers to another person. This includes Section 1028(a)(7) and both provisions of Section 1028A(a), which all refer to actions relating to "a means of identification of another person." The terrorism offense under Section 1028A(a)(2) is the only one of the three that also applies to the use of false identification documents.

CHAPTER 8
STATE IDENTITY THEFT LAWS

The American economy runs on credit, so identity theft can cause a lot of problems. Someone with good credit can quickly become someone with bad credit if an identity thief opens accounts in their name and doesn't pay the bills. Identity theft is a pervasive modern threat in part because of data insecurity issues. In addition to the federal identity theft law discussed in the previous chapter, each state also addresses some version of the crime. Attorneys who practice in multiple states should note that there are a lot of small differences between state identity theft laws that could have an impact on the outcome of a case. Is it enough for there to be possession of information you're not supposed to have? What about possession of information with the intent to use it to do something unlawful? Or is it not identity theft until the information is actually used?

The primary focus of identity theft laws is information. Why was the information obtained? How was the information used? Identity theft laws are especially concerned with PII, which depending on who you ask, either stands for personally identifiable information, personally identifying information, or personal identifying information. States vary a bit on what they consider to be PII. Some include biometric information in their definitions, while others do not. There is a lot of overlap between cyber-relevant laws, and the definition of personal information for identity theft purposes is often similar to how personal information is viewed in the respective state's data breach law.

State identity theft laws vary widely, so this chapter will primarily concern key categories of differences. For example, when defining the offense of identity theft, states use a lot of different verbs. In provisions that concern actions taken with data or identification documents, those verbs might include take, obtain, possess, manufacture, record, and use. Often, a clause about the perpetrator "verbing" identifying information or documents will be accompanied by a description of the perpetrator's future intent. This is especially likely when there are what we consider "lower action" baseline verbs. For example, Section 609.527 of the Minnesota Statutes says that identity theft occurs when a person "transfers, possesses, or uses an identity that is not the person's own, with the intent to commit, aid, or abet any unlawful activity." Possess is what we consider to be a lower action verb because it turns the identity theft statute into a quasi-inchoate offense. Note the distinction between using information for an unlawful purpose and possessing information with the intent to use that information for an unlawful purpose.

To demonstrate, we will describe the different parts of Ohio's identity theft law, which is one of the broader laws that we analyzed. In Ohio, the offense includes possessing personally identifying information with the intent to pretend to be that person. This possession with the intent to pretend standard is arguably lower than the more common possession with intent to defraud standard. Ohio's law also includes accomplice liability. Additionally, while the majority of states emphasize that the subject of the personal information did not consent to its use, Ohio actually recognizes an offense in letting someone borrow your personal information with the intent to defraud. The person who is borrowing information with the intent to defraud is also an offender under the Ohio law.

I. NAMES AND TYPES OF IDENTITY THEFT LAWS

Every state recognizes the crime of identity theft, though the terminology varies. States may vary, for instance, on whether they refer to the offense as identity fraud or identity theft. Federal identity theft law essentially uses both. Section 1028A of the federal law refers to "aggravated identity theft," and the primary offense is "fraud and related activity in connection with identification documents." It bears consideration how states classify their identity theft laws, whether as identity theft or identity fraud, or as some other variation. The Nebraska statutory code recognizes identity theft and identity fraud separately. In Nebraska, identity theft occurs when the perpetrator acquires real or fake identifying information with the intent to use that identity for an unlawful purpose. Identity fraud, on the other hand, occurs when the perpetrator 1) creates or alters identification documents, or 2) obtains personal identification documents "for any purpose of deception." The distinction that Nebraska makes between obtaining information (identity theft) and obtaining documents (identity fraud) is a hair that most states don't split, instead choosing a variation of one of the two terms.

The natures of the offenses covered by state identity theft laws are typically similar. Many emphasize the use of information. California has two different offenses—unauthorized use of personal identifying information and performance of certain acts in false character (which is similar to criminal impersonation). North Dakota also prohibits the unauthorized use of personal identifying information. Idaho refers to the misappropriation of personal identifying information. Maine classifies theirs as misuse of identification. Nevada has several offenses, all of which have vague names, but can be best described as "identity impersonation" and "public employee identity theft," both of which have varying degrees of severity. Rhode Island has the specific offense of obtaining property by false pretenses or personation. West Virginia recognizes the offense of taking the identity of another person.

Our main interest in discussing identity theft is to bring awareness to the data security angles and the effects on victims, but some state identity theft laws apply even when a fake persona is adopted. This raises a basic statutory analysis question: Who is the identity theft statute designed to protect?

Indiana prohibits both identity deception and synthetic identity deception. Indiana is the only state that currently uses the "synthetic" qualifier, though some other states emphasize that their identity theft laws apply to the use of both real and fictitious identities. In Oregon, Section 165.813 pertains to the unlawful possession of fictitious identification documents. Many states also note in their laws that identity theft prohibitions apply to the use of truthful identification information regardless of whether the data subject is living or deceased. This includes Section 817.568(8) of the Florida identity theft statute, which prohibits the fraudulent use of information belonging to deceased individuals and dissolved business entities. Texas also includes deceased individuals as possible identity theft targets, and Section 32.51 of the Texas Penal Code includes a stillborn infant or fetus as a deceased natural person for the purpose of the identity theft law.

There is some variation in how states approach criminal impersonation. In Alaska, criminal impersonation is the term applied to an offender possessing and using another person's identification documents as their own. In other states, criminal impersonation includes pretending to be someone in a position of authority or trust. For example, in addition to a separate identity fraud offense, Arkansas recognizes criminal impersonation, which involves either pretending to be a law enforcement officer or using a vehicle with such emblems as to make it appear to be law enforcement.[1] In New York, it is second degree criminal impersonation to pretend to be a public servant,[2] and first degree criminal impersonation to pretend to be a law enforcement

---

[1]   A.C.A. § 5–37–208.

[2]   N.Y. Penal Law § 190.23.

officer.[3] In some states, including Illinois and Tennessee, the criminal impersonation law extends to pretending to be a member of the armed services, similar to the federal Stolen Valor Act.

II. INTENT

Identity theft laws typically turn on what the perpetrator intended to do, like if the perpetrator acted with the intent to defraud. In a majority of states, the identity theft laws refer to the perpetrator having some intent to defraud or deceive. Many states prohibit the use of another's identity to aid in the commission of crimes, while others refer broadly to actions with "unlawful purpose." South Carolina's financial identity fraud statute includes the intent of "unlawfully devising a scheme or artifice to defraud."[4] Nebraska's identity fraud statute refers separately to actions with the intent to deceive and actions committed "for any purpose of deception."

Many states get more specific. Instead of just referring to an intent to defraud, laws often specify what the perpetrator was trying to achieve through identity theft. Connecticut's identity theft law includes the intent to "obtain or attempt to obtain money, credit, goods, services, property or medical information."[5] New Jersey's identity theft law prohibits identity theft for the purpose of obtaining benefits or services, or for avoiding payment for prior

---

[3]   N.Y. Penal Law § 190.25.

[4]   S.C. Code Ann. § 16–13–510(B)(2).

[5]   Conn. Gen. Stat. § 53a–129a(a).

services.[6] Washington D.C.'s identity theft law addresses the perpetrator's intent to obtain property, which is broadly defined to include real property, personal property, services, credit, debt, and government benefits.[7]

Many state identity theft laws include quasi-inchoate offenses, in the sense that identity theft occurs when a low-action activity like possession is combined with an intent to do something unlawful. Twenty-seven states use language similar to "possession with the intent to defraud" in delineating some aspects of offenses involving the collection of personal information. Some of these states also prohibit obtaining information with the intent to defraud, a low-action activity that occurs at an arguably earlier stage than possession. Eleven states prohibit the possession of identity theft tools with the intent to use those tools or facilitate the use of the tools by someone else to do something unlawful. In New Mexico, the possession of payment cards that the perpetrator knows were lost or misdelivered is a misdemeanor if the perpetrator intends to use the card or sell it to someone other than the actual cardholder or issuer.

The broadest possession-based identity theft statute in the country is probably Section 817.5685 in the Florida code. That provision prohibits the knowing, unauthorized possession of personal identification information of another person in any

---

6   N.J. Stat. § 2C:21–17(a).

7   D.C. Code § 22–3227.02(2); D.C. Code § 22–3227.01(4); D.C. Code § 22–3201(3).

form. There is no future intent requirement. Florida defines personal identification information as including things like social security numbers, government-issued identification numbers, financial account numbers, and medical records. In Florida, possession of the information of five or more individuals will support an inference that possession was knowing, intentional, and unauthorized. There are similar laws in other states, but none are as broad as Florida's law. California recognizes the offense of possession of actual identification documents, and Maryland prohibits the possession of fictitious or fraudulently altered identification documents. Pennsylvania prohibits the possession of an access device "knowing that it is counterfeit, altered, incomplete or belongs to another person who has not authorized its possession." Florida's law is not limited to access devices or documents, but rather applies when the personal identification information is possessed "in any form."

In some states, identity theft laws require some type of action with the information. Twenty-one states prohibit using identifying information in an attempt to obtain some sort of benefit. Some states use broader language about using or intending to use identifying information to commit a crime or for some other unlawful purpose.

Gains sought through the unauthorized use of another's information are often not pecuniary. There are several states that also include obtaining employment using someone else's identity. In Arizona and Georgia, violating the identity theft law with that kind of intent turns the act into aggravated identity theft.[8] Several states, including New Jersey and South Carolina, prohibit the use of another's identifying information to evade detection by law enforcement. In Virginia, it is unlawful to use another's identity "to avoid summons, arrest, prosecution, or to impede a criminal investigation." North Carolina refers broadly to actions with "the purpose of avoiding legal consequences." Alabama recognizes the crime of obstructing justice using a false identity, which roughly mirrors other laws about using another identity to avoid arrest.

The victim's economic resources might be negatively impacted, such as if a thief uses a stolen credit card number. In many cases, though, the victim may not experience any economic loss. None of the states require victims to experience economic loss for identity theft to be redressible. In their identity theft statutes, Arizona and New York both refer to a victim's economic loss as a factor, but showing economic loss is not the only way to establish identity theft in those states.

III. FALSE PERSONATION

False personation or criminal impersonation is often tangential to state identity theft laws. Many of these laws are about pretending to be someone else to obtain information. For example, Illinois and Nevada are two of the states that prohibit pretending to be another person in order to get information about

---

[8]   Arizona: A.R.S. § 13–2009(A)(3); Georgia: O.C.G.A. § 16–9–121.1(a).

that person. Montana considers that type of behavior to be a criminal invasion of personal privacy. North Dakota and Oklahoma prohibit using another's information to obtain the personally identifying information of another person, though it is not clear from the statutory language if that is limited to attempting to obtain information about the person the perpetrator is imitating. Some states criminalize pretending to be a representative of another person or organization to obtain something. In New York, it is considered false personation to lie to police about your name, date of birth, or address.

Many of the criminal impersonation laws are more about pretending to be a type of person rather than pretending to be a specific person. New York criminalizes lying to the police about one's identity, and also recognizes criminal impersonation in the first degree as including the act of pretending to be a police officer. So if Frank lies about his identity to Officer Bob, but Bob is actually only impersonating a police officer, Frank and Bob both have the necessary mens rea for their respective offenses. Since Frank's belief was mistaken, though, Bob is probably the only one in legal jeopardy.

There is some overlap between identity theft and criminal impersonation, but the overlap is not total. We would not consider it identity theft for a perpetrator to pretend to be a law enforcement official to manipulate other people, but several states treat the offenses as if they are related. The offenses do have similar themes of deception and manipulation. Sometimes there are crossovers, as in the case of statutes that address the impersonation of members of the armed services. New York's identity theft law recognizes aggravated identity theft as an offense that includes obtaining things by pretending to be a specific member of the armed services that the perpetrator knows is currently deployed. In 2018, Tennessee amended its criminal impersonation statute to include pretending to be a member of the armed services to obtain a tangible benefit.

Some states recognize online impersonation as a separate offense. In California, there is a law that prohibits "credible impersonation[s] of actual person[s]" online. In Michigan, it is a crime to use email to pretend to be part of a business in order to commit a crime.[9] New York similarly prohibits pretending to be someone online in order to obtain a benefit or defraud someone. New York also punishes online impersonation of "public servants" with the goal of using that identity to assert authority.

IV. ASSOCIATED OFFENSES

a.   TRAFFICKING IN STOLEN IDENTITIES

Many states criminalize additional activities related to identity theft. The most popular associated offense is trafficking in stolen identities. Ten states have some sort of version of this offense.[10] Tennessee refers to its version as "identity theft trafficking,"[11]

---

[9]   Mich. Comp. Laws Serv. § 445.67.

[10]   AL, AZ, CT, KS, KY, MI, MO, NJ, NC, TN.

[11]   Tenn. Code Ann. § 39–14–150(C)(1).

Kentucky's version of the offense is called "trafficking in financial information,"[12] and Kansas's version is named "dealing in false identification documents."[13]

Kansas defines an identification document to include credit or debit cards, "drivers' licenses, nondrivers' identification cards, certified copies of birth, death, marriage and divorce certificates, social security cards and employee identification cards."[14] Alabama and New Jersey also define identification documents for their statutes, with Alabama being one of the few states to list passports as a form of identification document.[15]

Alabama, Missouri, and North Carolina all require the intent that the trafficked information or documents be used to commit identity theft. Connecticut and Michigan require the intent to commit any crime, while Kentucky provides this intent as one option. Tennessee requires the intent to sell the means of identification.

As the act, Alabama, Kentucky, Missouri, and New Jersey all include the manufacturing, distribution, or possession of any item with personal identification information. Arizona, Connecticut, Kansas, Michigan, North Carolina, and Tennessee require that the actor knowingly sell or transfer the personal identification information of another, although Tennessee also includes the possession of the

---

12   Ky. Rev. Stat. Ann. § 434.874.

13   Kan. Stat. Ann. § 21–5918.

14   Kan. Stat. Ann. § 21–5918(e).

15   Ala. Code § 13A–8–191(1).

information. New Jersey and Tennessee both require the knowledge that the person purchasing the information or document is facilitating fraud or injury. Tennessee requires that the actor should have known as well.

The punishments for these statutes vary widely. Alabama's statute[16] provides for the harshest punishment, as an offender faces an authorized imprisonment of 2–20 years for the Class B felony. The statute also provides for a maximum fine of $30,000. Arizona provides for the highest possible fine, as it is a Class 2 felony with a maximum fine of $150,000 and an authorized imprisonment of 4–10 years. Arizona can also give a maximum probationary period of seven years.

Connecticut classifies this offense as a Class D felony with a maximum fine of $5,000 and a maximum authorized imprisonment of five years. Kansas classifies it as a severity level 8 nonperson felony with an authorized imprisonment of 9–11 months. Kentucky classifies it as a Class C felony with an authorized imprisonment of 5–10 years. Michigan provides for a maximum fine of $25,000 and a maximum authorized imprisonment of five years. Missouri classifies the offense as a Class B felony with an authorized imprisonment of 5–15 years.

New Jersey classifies the offense originally as a crime of the fourth degree, with a maximum fine of $10,000 and a maximum authorized imprisonment of

---

[16]   Ala. Code § 13A–8–193.

eighteen months. If the actor traffics twenty or more items or five or more items from five or more victims, it is a crime of the third degree with a maximum fine of $15,000 with an authorized imprisonment of 3–5 years. If fifty or more items are trafficked or ten or more items from five or more victims, it becomes a crime of the second degree with a maximum fine of $150,000 and an authorized imprisonment of 5–10 years.

North Carolina classifies the offense as a Class E felony, which provides an authorized imprisonment of 15–63 months. Tennessee classifies the offense as a Class C felony with a maximum fine of $10,000 and an authorized imprisonment of 3–15 years.

b.   FACILITATING IDENTITY THEFT

Trafficking is one type of offense where a third party can be liable based on their contribution to someone else's criminal activity. Many states also address the possession and use of identity theft tools, often with separate provisions addressing the use of skimmers and re-encoders to steal financial account information and transfer that information to a blank card. A criminal might install a skimmer on a gas pump's credit card reader. By doing this, the criminal can capture card data without stealing the physical card. Generally, state laws about such tools require possession of the tools with the intent that the tools be used unlawfully, but in Florida, possession of skimmers is a felony, with no language about future intent.

A few states impose liability on a third party who accepts personal information that they know is false. Georgia recognizes "identity fraud by receipt of fraudulent identification information."[17] Arizona recognizes the crime of "knowingly accepting the identity of another person," which targets employers who knowingly accept false identification information to verify employment eligibility. Idaho prohibits the possession of goods or cash that the perpetrator should know were obtained through identity theft.[18]

Three states also address some records disposal aspects of identity theft. Illinois has a statute for facilitating identity theft.[19] For example, consider Ralph, a government clerk with access to personally identifying information as part of his job. The Illinois statute makes it an offense for Ralph to dispose of that information without somehow destroying it, if this is done "knowingly, with the intent of committing identity theft, aggravated identity theft, or any violation of the Illinois Financial Crime Law." Ralph would probably not be in legal trouble under that provision for negligently throwing away a bunch of papers without special destruction of sensitive information.

Illinois stands out for its inclusion of a criminal provision relating to records disposal. Elsewhere, records disposal requirements are generally treated

---

[17]   Ga. Code § 16–9–121(b).

[18]   Idaho Code § 18–3127.

[19]   720 ILCS 5/16–32.

as regulatory infractions. In Michigan, those who maintain databases of personal information must completely remove and destroy information about an individual when that individual is removed from the database.[20] Tennessee likewise requires the responsible destruction of personal information that is no longer to be kept. In Tennessee, a violation of this provision is considered a violation of the state consumer protection act.[21]

As liability expands outward from the most direct wrongdoer, states generally require facilitators to be similarly culpable compared to the identity thief who uses the stolen information. Generally, the mens rea required for identity theft is intentionally, knowingly, or willfully. Very few states recognize recklessness as supporting liability for identity theft as a primary or facilitating offense. Under Alabama's Consumer Identity Protection Act, consumer reporting agencies can be held civilly liable if the agencies behave recklessly in failing to comply with a consumer's request to block any changes to their credit information caused by the identity theft. In Alaska, criminal impersonation in the first degree requires that the perpetrator has recklessly damaged the victim's financial reputation. In Vermont, it is a crime for a person to recklessly facilitate identity theft by someone else.[22] Delaware is the only state where a mens rea of recklessness will support the primary crime of identity theft, because that law

---

[20]   Mich. Comp. Laws § 445.72a, Sec. 12a.

[21]   Tenn. Code Ann. § 39–14–150(g).

[22]   Vt. Stat. Ann. tit. 13, § 2030.

refers to recklessly possessing information. However, even if the possession of personal information is "reckless," the possession must still be with the intent to commit a crime.[23]

V. PUNISHMENT

State justice systems vary significantly in how they grade offenses and what confinement sentences or fines may be imposed. States use different criteria for determining sentencing and offense grading, so comparing states on specific points is inefficient. Identity theft offenses can be misdemeanors or felonies, and often the difference can depend on who the victim or perpetrator is.

Many states recognize factors that can increase the punishment range. In the majority of states, punishment can be affected by the value obtained by the perpetrator, the value lost by the victim, or the number of victims. About a quarter of states recognize an enhanced identity theft offense when the victim is a senior citizen or a member of another vulnerable group.

Nevada has a separate offense for identity theft by a public employee.[24] Both types of identity theft are category B felonies, but violations of 205.464 have a minimum prison term of five years compared to a minimum prison term of one year for the more general identity theft law in 205.463. Moreover, under Nevada's general identity theft law, identity

---

[23] 11 Del.C. § 854.

[24] Nev. Rev. Stat. Ann. § 205.464.

theft violations against senior citizens have a minimum prison term of three years, compared to a minimum prison term of seven years if the perpetrator is a public employee who violated 205.464. In addition to the vulnerability of the target, other factors that might increase the minimum prison sentence include the number of victims affected and the economic harm suffered by the victim.

VI. COMPENSATION FOR VICTIMS

Three main types of victim compensation will be discussed in this section: identity theft passports, restitution, and civil remedies. Identity theft victims are also benefited by laws that impose requirements on credit reporting agencies. Alabama, Virginia, and New Jersey require these agencies to block items from a consumer's credit profile that were added because of identity theft. Delaware and Montana require credit reporting agencies to accept an identity theft passport as notice of a dispute. West Virginia addresses requirements for credit reporting agencies when a consumer requests a security freeze. Such freezes allow consumers to block new activities in their credit report. Consumers can then unfreeze their credit later as needed. West Virginia is among a handful of states that address security freezes in their statutes relevant to identity theft. Credit agencies previously charged for security freezes, and some state identity theft laws set limits on the fees that could be charged for a security freeze. As of September of 2018, federal law requires credit agencies to provide security freezes to customers at no charge. This requirement was added as part of the Economic Growth, Regulatory Relief, and Consumer Protection Act passed by Congress in 2018.

Ten states allow victims to apply for an identity theft passport.[25] Nevada has an "identity theft program card" that seems to serve the same purpose as an identity theft passport. Eight of the ten states (Virginia and New Mexico exempted) require identity theft victims to file a police report before they can apply for an identity theft passport. Approved applications are forwarded to the state Attorney General, who then issues the identity theft passport to the victim.

A victim may present an identity theft passport to a law enforcement agency "to help prevent the victim's arrest or detention for an offense committed by someone other than the victim who is using the victim's identity."[26] This is similar to provisions in other identity theft laws that address a victim's right to have court records edited to reflect their factual innocence if a crime was committed using their information. In Oklahoma, those kinds of expungements can be used to get an identity theft passport. Identity theft passports can also be shared with creditors and credit reporting agencies as notification of potentially fraudulent charges.

There are some limitations on who can obtain an identity theft passport. Iowa requires the victim to be a citizen of the state or a victim of identity theft in

---

25   DE, IA, MD, MS, MT, NV, NM, OH, OK, VA.

26   Del. Code Ann. tit. 11, § 854A(b)(1).

the state of Iowa in order to get an identity theft passport.[27] Nevada law states that a Nevada resident can file a report with a law enforcement agency in any state, but a nonresident who is a victim in Nevada must file a report in the state.[28]

Most states do not use the tool of identity theft passports. Instead, states often address what costs the victims of identity theft may seek reimbursement for. A majority of state identity theft laws address restitution for identity theft victims. This may include attorney fees, costs of credit monitoring, or the cost of replacing checks, among others. In ten states, identity theft laws create a civil cause of action for the victim.[29] Three other states create a civil cause of action in limited circumstances. South Carolina recognizes a right of action available to victims of identity fraud enabling unlawful presence, but not for regular identity fraud. California and Wyoming recognize a private right of action for violations of the respective state's online impersonation law.

Many identity theft laws increase penalties or offense grades based on the identity of the victim. Thirteen states impose harsher punishment when the victim was a senior citizen. Some state laws about impersonation become higher level offenses if the person impersonated was a law enforcement officer or a member of the armed services.

---

27   Iowa Code § 715A.9A(1)(a).

28   Nev. Rev. Stat. § 205.4651(1)(a), (b).

29   AL, CA, GA, IL, MO, NJ, OK, SC, VA.

Ten states provide a process for how identity theft victims can request for court records to be amended to reflect the victim's factual innocence in prosecutions against the identity thief that used the victim's information. Six of these, Alabama, California, Illinois, North Carolina, Utah, and Wyoming, do not also have identity theft passport programs. Mississippi, Montana, Nevada, and Virginia all provide for this process for changing court records, and they also have a system similar or equivalent to identity theft passports.

This summary of identity theft laws demonstrates that small linguistic choices by legislators ("using information to defraud" versus "possessing information with the intent to use it to defraud") potentially make a significant difference in how the same behavior is prosecuted across state lines.

CHAPTER 9

RECENT CHANGES TO FEDERAL CYBERSECURITY LAW

The discovery of Stuxnet in 2010 provided a wake-up call for the computer security industry, critical infrastructure providers, the general public, and basically anyone who was not already involved in the creation and dissemination of the Stuxnet worm. Eventually, discussions resulted in a variety of largely incremental changes in national cybersecurity policy. The first of these was President Obama's Executive Order 13,636, which is titled Improving Critical Infrastructure Cybersecurity. The Order's most significant contribution to cybersecurity policy was arguably its direction to develop the Cybersecurity Framework. In the years since the order was signed, the Cybersecurity Framework has become a resource for security professionals outside of critical infrastructure as well. EO 13,636 was complemented by Presidential Policy Directive 21 (PPD-21), which addressed the various roles of government agencies in the implementation of EO 13,636. Multiple cybersecurity-related bills were enacted in December 2014, and the federal Cybersecurity Information Sharing Act was enacted as part of an omnibus budget bill in December 2015. We start with an explanation of EO 13,636 because it laid the foundation for later developments in the areas of cybersecurity standards and cyber threat information sharing.

I. EXECUTIVE ORDER 13,636, PRESIDENTIAL POLICY DIRECTIVE 21, AND THE CYBERSECURITY FRAMEWORK

Section 1 of EO 13,636 emphasizes that the Order's purpose is to address the growth of cyber risks affecting critical infrastructure systems while balancing the occasionally conflicting values of security and privacy. Section 1 of the Order underscores the administration's policy to enhance the security and resilience of critical infrastructure systems without sacrificing "business confidentiality, privacy, [or] civil liberties." In Section 2, the Order defines critical infrastructure as "systems and assets, whether physical or virtual, so vital to the United States that the incapacity or destruction of such systems and assets would have a debilitating impact on security, national economic security, national public health or safety, or any combination of those matters." This is also the definition for critical infrastructure adopted in the Homeland Security Act. Section 3 of the Order directs agencies to coordinate on issues relating to the Order using an established interagency process, the National Security Council System.

Section 4 sets out the guidelines for cybersecurity information sharing. The emphasis of Section 4 is to make sure that the government can easily share classified cyber threat information with critical infrastructure providers in the private sector. Section 5 is about the privacy and civil liberties protections for disclosed information, which the Order requires to be based on the eight Fair Information Practice

Principles (FIPPs) listed in the National Strategy for Trusted Identities in Cyberspace. Under the FIPPs, 1) organizations must provide transparency about how the organization handles personally identifiable information (PII), 2) there must be process for individuals to participate in the organization's handling of PII, 3) organizations must explain under what authority they are collecting the PII and why, 4) organizations must limit PII collection to the amount necessary for the specified purpose, 5) organizations must limit use of PII to the amount and kind of use necessary for the specified purpose, 6) organizations must protect PII to maintain data quality and integrity, 7) organizations must have appropriate security safeguards for PII to protect against unauthorized access or use, and 8) organizations must have processes for accountability and auditing to ensure future compliance with the FIPPs. Put in more bullet point friendly terms, the eight FIPPs are

1. Transparency
2. Individual participation
3. Purpose specification
4. Data minimization
5. Use limitation
6. Data quality and integrity
7. Security
8. Accountability and auditing[1]

---

[1]   Privacy Policy Guidance Memorandum No. 2008-01 from Hugo Teufel III, Chief Privacy Officer, U.S. Dep't of Homeland

The FTC also has its own idea of fair information practices. The FTC's approach is more consumer-driven than that of DHS. The FTC views FIPs as being based on five core principles: (1) notice and consumer awareness; (2) consumer choice and consent; (3) access and participation in the process; (4) data integrity and security; and (5) enforcement and redress.[2]

In Section 7, EO 13,636 instructs the National Institute of Standards and Technology to develop a Cybersecurity Framework (CSF), to be used as a voluntary cybersecurity standard that can be adopted by private entities. NIST completed the task, and the CSF is available on NIST's website. Section 10 concerns the process for adoption of the CSF.

The CSF was designed as a voluntary cybersecurity standard to be used by critical infrastructure service providers, but the structure of the CSF is adaptable to other industries as well. The CSF uses a risk-based framework that is divided into five core functions: Identify, Protect, Detect, Respond, and Recover. Each function is subdivided into categories and subcategories. The Identify core function emphasizes efforts to identify potential issues in advance. For example, Asset Management and Risk Assessment are two of the categories within

---

Sec., on The Fair Information Practice Principles: Framework for Privacy Policy at the Dep't of Homeland Security 1 (Dec. 29, 2008), *available at* http://www.dhs.gov/xlibrary/assets/privacy/privacy_policyguide_2008-01.pdf.

[2]   Federal Trade Commission, Report to Congress, https://www.ftc.gov/sites/default/files/documents/reports/privacy-online-report-congress/priv-23a.pdf.

the Identify core function. The Protect core function is about prevention, and categories include Protective Technology and Maintenance. The Detect core function addresses steps to ensure that cybersecurity events are detected within a reasonable time. One category within the Detect core function is Security Continuous Monitoring. The Respond core function has categories that include Analysis and Mitigation. The Recover core function is about the resilience of systems, and Recovery Planning is one of its categories.

Section 8 provides the outline for agency support of the critical infrastructure cybersecurity program. Agencies that are designated Sector-Specific Agencies are important contact points for private sector businesses in various industries. Finally, Section 9 of EO 13,636 requires the identification of critical infrastructure providers that are at the greatest risk of a cybersecurity incident causing catastrophic consequences.

PPD-21 focuses on three strategic imperatives. The first strategic imperative emphasizes the need to unify efforts across the federal government relating to the protection of critical infrastructure. To further this goal, PPD-21 requires DHS to operate two critical infrastructure centers: one to focus on physical infrastructure, and one to focus on cyber infrastructure. The second strategic imperative focuses on baseline data and systems requirements to ensure format uniformity, interoperability, and redundancy to ensure continued access if there is a disruption. The third strategic imperative is to use data analysis to inform decisions regarding critical infrastructure, including ongoing analysis of incidents, threats, and emerging risks, to provide "a near real-time situational awareness capability."

SSAs are a significant focus of PPD-21. Under the directive, SSAs are defined as the department or agency that is designated to work with a specific critical infrastructure sector on their security and resilience programs. PPD-21 identifies sixteen critical infrastructure sectors. Of the sixteen, DHS is listed as the sole SSA for eight sectors and is a co-SSA for two additional sectors. DHS is often an important actor in cybersecurity policy discussions. The National Cybersecurity Protection Act of 2014, which we discuss later, references the situational awareness and sector-specific agency language of PPD-21, which suggests that in passing the NCPA, Congress intended to formalize a number of elements of PPD-21.

a.   EO 13,636 AND PPD-21

EO 13,636 and PPD-21 each require multiple annual reports. Section 5(b) of EO 13,636 requires an annual review of the report on privacy and civil-liberties risks associated with the program,[3] and sections 8 and 9 each require an annual report pertaining to critical infrastructure found to be at greatest risk.[4] Under Section 8(c), the SSAs are required to report annually to the President about

---

[3]   Exec. Order No. 13,636, § 5(b), 78 Fed. Reg. at 11,740.

[4]   *Id.* §§ 8(c), 9(a), 78 Fed. Reg. at 11,742.

the program participation by owners and operators of critical infrastructure at greatest risk, and under Section 9(a), the list of critical infrastructure at greatest risk shall be reviewed and updated annually. PPD-21 also preserves the obligation of the Secretary of Homeland Security to submit annual reports "on the status of national critical infrastructure" and also requires SSAs to provide annual reports to support the Secretary in the preparation of his annual reports.

II. LEGISLATIVE ACTIONS

In December 2014, Congress passed three cybersecurity-related bills, which were all signed by President Obama on December 18, 2014: 1) the Federal Information Security Modernization Act of 2014 (FISMA),[5] 2) the National Cybersecurity Protection Act of 2014 (NCPA),[6] and 3) the Cybersecurity Enhancement Act of 2014 (CEA).[7] FISMA is an update to the older Federal Information Security Management Act, and focuses on the cybersecurity practices of federal agencies.[8] FISMA is also briefly discussed in the privacy chapter later in this text.

NCPA codifies the functions of the National Cybersecurity and Communications Integration Center (NCCIC) of the Department of Homeland

---

[5]   P.L. 113–283 (2014).

[6]   P.L. 113–282 (2014).

[7]   P.L. 113–274 (2014).

[8]   P.L. 113–283; *see also* 44 U.S.C. § 3551 et seq.

Security (DHS).[9] The NCPA approaches cybersecurity from an information-sharing perspective, though the NCPA only allows the government to share information and does not address cybersecurity information held by the private sector.[10] The NCCIC is authorized to facilitate information-sharing agreements for cybersecurity purposes.

The CEA addresses a variety of topics like cybersecurity research and education, but for current purposes, its most significant contribution is Title I, which sets forth detailed guidance for the National Institute for Standards and Technology's activities relating to cybersecurity standards. Through this Title, the CEA provides legislative oversight of the CSF.

Much of the formal legislative action has emphasized critical infrastructure. EO 13,636 used the term "critical infrastructure" as defined by the Homeland Security Act, but Presidential Policy Directive 21 (PPD-21) narrowed this term by specifically enumerating the sectors that would be covered. The CEA and NCPA similarly use the term "critical infrastructure," and the CEA also includes the limiting "sector-specific agency" language of PPD-21.

In December 2015, Congress enacted the Cybersecurity Information Sharing Act (CISA) as part of the omnibus budget bill for 2016. CISA's

---

[9]   P.L. 113–282.

[10]   P.L. 113–282 at § 3.

primary focus is the creation of a model for bidirectional cyber threat information sharing between the government and private sector. CISA and the CEA are both codified in the Cybersecurity chapter of Title 6.

Title I of CISA creates an information sharing program to make it easier for the government to share cyber threat information with the private sector, and vice versa. CISA defines "cybersecurity threat" as an action "that may result in an unauthorized effort to adversely impact the security, availability, confidentiality, or integrity of an information system or information that is stored on, processed by, or transiting an information system." Most of the provisions of CISA concern the sharing of "cyber threat indicators," which are defined as information that describes or identifies a variety of things relating to security, including "a method of causing a user with legitimate access to an information system . . . to unwittingly enable the defeat of a security control or exploitation of a security vulnerability." Another type of cyber threat indicator is malicious reconnaissance, which is "a method for actively probing or passively monitoring an information system for the purpose of discerning security vulnerabilities of the information, if such method is associated with a known or suspected cybersecurity threat." Security vulnerabilities are broadly defined as "any attribute of hardware, software, process, or procedure that could enable or facilitate the defeat of a security control."

a.   CISA AND THE FIRST AMENDMENT

A careful reading of how "cyber threat indicator" is defined in CISA reveals a potential conflict with the First Amendment. One such indicator that can be shared is information about a method for causing a legitimate operator to "unwittingly enable the defeat of a security control." If this were limited to technological methods, there might be less concern because by its language, this definition would most clearly refer to phishing attacks. As written, however, CISA potentially enables prosecutions where the investigation was triggered because someone shared information about social engineering. The definition of security vulnerabilities as including processes and procedures supports this interpretation.

Social engineering is a major part of hacking. While the movies often make hacking look like it consists of endless technical jargon and countless hours in front of a screen, real hacking often involves collecting personal information or even passwords by posing as someone who is authorized to receive that information. By sweeping information about social engineering into the definition of "cyber threat indicators," CISA raises concerns about unlawful advocacy and the First Amendment.

Unlawful advocacy is an issue that emerges in First Amendment jurisprudence about informational speech. Informational speech cases are tricky in part because some types of information may have beneficial uses as well as harmful uses. In the context of cybersecurity, information about vulnerabilities can help defenders shore up their systems, or it can enable attackers to develop new attack methods. Such information is often presented at information security conferences. Information security conferences attract thousands of security professionals, and most of the people at exploit demonstrations are likely more interested in learning about possible threats than about actually exploiting vulnerabilities for personal gain. Regardless, public presentations nonetheless raise the danger that malicious actors will use the information for harmful purposes.

As noted above, CISA's language is also potentially broad enough to encompass social engineering practices. A teenager supposedly hacked into CIA Director John Brennan's personal AOL email account through social engineering instead of through the use of complicated tools. After discovering that Brennan was a Verizon customer, the teenager claims that he and a friend contacted Verizon and pretended to be a Verizon technician who could not obtain a customer's records because of a computer problem. By doing this, the hackers obtained several different types of personal information about Brennan, including the last four digits of Brennan's bank card. He then used this information to reset the password for Brennan's AOL account and explore the contents of Brennan's personal email. Over the course of three days, Brennan reclaimed his account three times, and the hackers retook Brennan's account three times, before Brennan finally deleted his AOL account entirely.

The description of the hacker's social engineering technique is easily "information about a method," satisfying one of the thresholds for being a cyber threat indicator. By revealing sensitive customer information to the hackers, the Verizon employees clearly "unwittingly enable[d] the defeat of a security control." By recounting the hacker's exploits, we have now communicated information that is authorized for collection and sharing under CISA. This element of CISA could easily chill speech. It is no secret that the most severe security flaws are generally located between the keyboard and the chair, but human security flaws are better addressed by organizational policies. Malicious social engineering is already addressed through criminal laws prohibiting fraud, and the potential for treating social engineering information as a cyber threat indicator is unnecessary and unhelpful.

b.   CISA, MALICIOUS RECONNAISSANCE, AND RESEARCH

Another type of cyber threat indicator under CISA is information about malicious reconnaissance. Malicious reconnaissance is not defined based on action, but rather as a method. It is malicious reconnaissance to probe or monitor an information system to find vulnerabilities "if such method is associated with a known or suspected cybersecurity threat." Note that the language refers to the method being associated with a suspected cybersecurity threat, with no limitation for the intent of the person searching for vulnerabilities. Security researchers typically use the same "methods" as malicious hackers for finding technological vulnerabilities, though they typically do not intend the sort of adverse impact required in the definition of "cyber threat." Declaring this behavior "malicious reconnaissance" could affect future choices of freelance security researchers.

Hackers are often described using three shades: white hat hackers, grey hat hackers, and black hat hackers. White hat hackers are typically security researchers who work directly for the company whose products they are checking for vulnerabilities. Black hat hackers are on the other side of the spectrum, typically intending to cause mischief. In the middle are the grey hat hackers, who might identify vulnerabilities in products and then offer to sell the information to the vendor. If the vendor is uninterested in purchasing the information, the hacker might sit on the information, or might look for another buyer, like a vulnerability reseller who sells vulnerabilities to governments.

Even though "malicious reconnaissance" suggests that malice should be a necessary element, the definition itself is too broad. By defining malicious reconnaissance based on methods and not based on action or intent, CISA potentially makes grey hat hackers subject to government compulsion as soon as they disclose to the company that they have information for sale. A company that wants the information but does not want to pay might report the communication to the government. The government investigates the hacker, and might compel the hacker to provide the information to the vendor at no cost, rendering the use of the hacker's time and expertise worthless. This sort of structure could cause some grey hat hackers to shift closer to the side of black hats, as the incentive for them to offer information for sale to vendors dissolves.

III. CRITICAL INFRASTRUCTURE AND CYBERSECURITY

Concern about critical infrastructure has driven developments in the federal law of cybersecurity over the last several years. Critical infrastructure systems often rely on supervisory control and data acquisition (SCADA) systems. Stuxnet exploited SCADA systems. It is possible that Stuxnet's discovery may have prompted more research to identify SCADA vulnerabilities. According to Symantec, there were fifteen publicly known SCADA vulnerabilities in 2010, and 129 publicly known SCADA vulnerabilities in 2011. Stuxnet was uncovered in 2010.

EO 13,636 also calls for DHS to propose possible incentives to promote participation in the voluntary cybersecurity program by critical infrastructure providers. The Order notes, however, that additional legislation might be required in order to implement some types of incentives. In terms of financial incentive, tax breaks when a company is found to be sufficiently adhering to the program *or* tax credits for the cost of implementing suggested controls may both be viable options. Another option is for the Cybersecurity Framework to exempt private entities from civil liability when the entity makes a good faith effort to comply with the Framework (an option discussed in general terms in a law review article by Trope and Humes).[11]

Statutory liability exemptions are not uncommon. There is one such exemption in the Stored Communications Act excusing electronic communication service providers from liability for sharing customer information.[12] The FISA Amendments Act of 2008 also provides release from liability for electronic communication service providers who provided information to comply with a directive issued by the Director of National Intelligence and the Attorney General.[13]

IV. ADMINISTRATIVE AGENCIES

Administrative agencies have also been involved in regulating cybersecurity to varying degrees. The Securities and Exchange Commission, for instance, has issued guidance documents about cybersecurity.[14] The guidance, which was updated in February 2018, emphasizes the significant impact that cybersecurity incidents can have on investor confidence, and reiterates that insider trading using non-public knowledge of a cybersecurity incident is against the law. In March 2018, the SEC charged a

---

[11]   Roland L. Trope and Stephen J. Humes, *Before Rolling Blackouts Begin: Briefing Boards on Cyber Attacks That Target and Degrade the Grid*, 40 WM. MITCHELL L. REV. 647 (2014).

[12]   18 U.S.C. § 2703(e) (2012).

[13]   50 U.S.C. § 1881a(h)(3) (2012).

[14]   Securities and Exchange Commission, Commission Statement and Guidance on Public Company Cybersecurity Disclosures, https://www.sec.gov/rules/interp/2018/33-10459.pdf (Feb. 26, 2018).

former Equifax executive with insider trading because the former executive sold a significant amount of Equifax stock between when Equifax discovered the 2017 data breach and when Equifax disclosed the data breach to the public.[15]

The Department of Homeland Security (DHS) operates the National Cybersecurity and Communications Integration Center to coordinate responses with the private and government sectors.[16] DHS also operates the Office of Cybersecurity and Communications to focus on critical information infrastructure.[17]

The Department of Health and Human Services has released guidance on the interplay between the NIST's Cybersecurity Framework and the HIPAA Security Rule.[18] DHHS's Office of Civil Rights acknowledged that the mapping was not perfect, but most function subcategories in the Cybersecurity Framework have one or more corresponding provisions in the Security Rule. For example, the

---

[15] Former Equifax Executive Charged with Insider Trading, SEC.gov, https://www.sec.gov/news/press-release/2018-40 (Mar. 14, 2018).

[16] Dept. of Homeland Sec., National Cybersecurity and Communications, DHS.gov, https://www.dhs.gov/national-cybersecurity-and-communications-integration-center.

[17] Office of Cybersecurity and Communications, Dep't of Homeland Sec., https://www.dhs.gov/office-cybersecurity-and-communications (last visited Dec. 20, 2016).

[18] Office for Civil Rights, Addressing Gaps in Cybersecurity: OCR Releases Crosswalk Between HIPAA Security Rule and NIST Cybersecurity Framework, HHS.gov, https://www.hhs.gov/hipaa/for-professionals/security/nist-security-hipaa-crosswalk/index.html (last visited Feb. 2, 2017).

Cybersecurity Framework's Identity function has a Risk Assessment category. One of the requirements within that category is that asset vulnerabilities must be identified and documented, which corresponds with HIPAA Security Rules 45 C.F.R. §§ .308(a)(1)(ii)(A), 164.308(a)(7)(ii)(E), 164.308(a)(8), 164.310(a)(1), 164.312(a)(1), and 164.316(b)(2)(iii).

The Federal Trade Commission has emerged as the primary administrative agency for addressing cybersecurity and privacy concerns. The FTC's authority is primarily derived from its authority to censure unfair or deceptive acts or practices by private companies. Section 5 of the FTC Act gives the FTC the authority to declare business practices to be unfair and thus unlawful if the practices cause "substantial injury" to consumers. Many FTC actions end in settlements or consent decrees. In August 2014, the FTC settled charges against Fandango and Credit Karma regarding the companies' failures to adequately secure sensitive information that customers submitted through their mobile applications.[19]

In 2015, the Third Circuit affirmed the FTC's authority in FTC v. Wyndham, concluding that the FTC may rightly consider a cybersecurity practice unfair when that practice has resulted in harm to

---

[19] Federal Trade Comm'n, FTC Approves Final Orders Settling Charges Against Fandango and Credit Karma, Press Release, Aug. 19, 2014, https://www.ftc.gov/news-events/press-releases/2014/08/ftc-approves-final-orders-settling-charges-against-fandango.

consumers.[20] Past consent decrees indicate that unfair cybersecurity practices include not protecting against "commonly known or reasonably foreseeable attacks from third parties," not encrypting data, not using an intrusion detection system, and not providing cybersecurity training to employees.[21]

Often, FTC adjudications lead to consent decrees that require ongoing monitoring, but the censured organization is not fined. In 2011, Facebook entered into a consent decree with the FTC that bars Facebook "from making misrepresentations about the privacy or security of consumers' personal information."[22] A violation of the consent decree could be punished by a fine of $40,000 per violation. As of this writing, the FTC is still evaluating Facebook's case.

---

[20]   F.T.C. v. Wyndham Worldwide Corp., 799 F.3d 236, 249 (3d Cir. 2015).

[21]   *E.g., In re* LabMD, Inc., Docket No. 9357, Opinion of the Commission, by Chairwoman Edith Ramirez, at 1, *available at* https://www.ftc.gov/system/files/documents/cases/160729labmd-opinion.pdf.

[22]   Press Release, Federal Trade Commission, Facebook Settles FTC Charges That It Deceived Consumers by Failing to Keep Privacy Promises (Nov. 29, 2011), https://www.ftc.gov/news-events/press-releases/2011/11/facebook-settles-ftc-charges-it-deceived-consumers-failing-keep.

CHAPTER 10

CYBERSECURITY AND INTERNATIONAL LAW

Borders don't mean much to data transfers. Legal practitioners have been making inroads into jurisdiction issues in Internet-related domestic cases. State cybercrime statutes often address jurisdiction issues specifically. When the relevant borders are international, the substantive legal issues can get very complicated.

This chapter focuses on international law.[1] A major role of international law is to govern relations between countries. With the rise of globalization, international law has continued to evolve. The Internet and the increasingly digital world pose new challenges. In this chapter, we focus on the aspects of international law that are implicated most significantly by these developments. This includes treaties, restrictions on dual use goods, protections for targets that serve military and non-military purposes, and how the law of war applies to cyber weapons. The EU's General Data Protection Regulation (GDPR) is addressed in a later chapter about privacy.

---

[1]   Portions of this chapter previously appeared in a chapter written by the authors and published in the International Encyclopedia of Digital Communication and Society (Wiley-Blackwell, 2015). Reproduced with permission. Some aspects of the chapter were also drawn from other law review articles written by the authors.

As we have previously noted, the law of cybersecurity is in flux, and discussions often draw from other areas of law. This challenge is especially pressing in the laws of war. In the context of cyberwar, what rules apply to these new weapons? The laws of war were shaped by physical interactions and threats. Whether it was arrows, swords, a trebuchet, an AK-47, biological weaponry, napalm, or a nuclear bomb, the threats of conventional weapons affected the physical environment, and it was generally easy to see when a weapon had been used. With cyber weapons, the points of ambiguity are seemingly endless. There is also currently some overlap between civilian and military information infrastructure, so even lawyers in the private sector can benefit from some awareness of the developing international law issues relating to cybersecurity.

I. INTERNATIONAL AGREEMENTS

To address the ambiguities in the international law of cyber weapons, one option is for nations to join together to draft a treaty. As defined in Article 38 of the Statute of the International Court of Justice, international treaties are one of the four sources of international law. The other three enumerated sources of international law are international custom, general principles of law that are recognized by civilized nations, and judicial decisions.

Article 2 of the Vienna Convention of the Law of Treaties defines a treaty as "an international agreement concluded between States in written form and governed by international law." A treaty may also be referred to by other terms, including an act, a protocol, a convention, or a declaration. The development of a treaty includes several stages. First, the content of the treaty is negotiated. Then, the final form of the treaty is adopted. Finally, once the treaty has been adopted, it is given force by the acceptance of the treaty by nations that consent to be bound. In some cases, the signing of the treaty may be sufficient to signify consent to be bound. In other situations, however, ratification may also be required, which requires the treaty also be approved by the parliamentary or legislative branch of the signatory's domestic government. A State that is not a signatory may also be able to become a party to the treaty by acceding to the terms of the treaty, likely by filing an instrument of accession.

a.   EXAMPLE—THE EUROPEAN CONVENTION ON CYBERCRIME

In the interest of developing a common criminal policy on the issue of cybercrime, the Council of Europe developed the European Convention on Cybercrime (ECC). The ECC was opened for signature on November 23, 2001. The terms of the ECC required at least five ratifications, three of which had to be by member states of the Council of Europe, before the treaty would be in force. The ECC entered into force as of July 1, 2004. As of 2018, 46 of the 47 countries in the Council of Europe have signed or ratified the ECC, with Russia being the only holdout country within the Council of Europe.

In addition to the 46 member signatories, 13 non-member States also signed, ratified, or acceded to the ECC: Australia, Canada, Chile, Dominican Republic, Israel, Japan, Mauritius, Panama, Senegal, South Africa, Sri Lanka, Tonga, and the United States. The existence of the ECC, even though it has not been broadly adopted, shows leaders' awareness that cybersecurity concerns transcend national boundaries.

The ECC is divided into four chapters and a preamble. The first chapter defines some key terms. The second chapter addresses measures that the participating countries should take at a national level. The first section of Chapter 2 is about standardizing substantive criminal laws across countries. The first category of laws covers offenses that compromise the confidentiality, integrity, and availability of data and systems. The ECC also requires participating countries to have criminal laws against computer-related forgery and fraud, child pornography, and intellectual property infringement. Other aspects of the ECC address procedural elements like data preservation, the collection of data during investigations, and jurisdiction. Chapter 3 of the ECC sets forth principles for international cooperation in cybercrime investigations. Chapter 4 of the ECC provides the final provisions for the adoption and application of the Convention.

b.   EXPORT CONTROLS

One issue relating to technology, international law, and commerce is the use of export restrictions. The United States government has a complicated system of statutes and regulations covering exports. While making online purchases, consumers sometimes notice a statement that the product they are ordering cannot be shipped outside of the United States. This kind of notice is frequently related to export controls. Export control regulations often focus on technologies that terrorists or hostile nations could use to harm the United States. Many such technologies are considered dual-use, in that they have both peaceful and offensive applications.

Encryption technology has long been considered a dual-use technology. Export regulations for encryption products in the United States have waxed and waned. Cryptography controls were first introduced by Congress in 1979.[2] Export restrictions on cryptography tools led to several incidents where researchers faced restrictions when attempting to present cryptography research at international conferences.[3] The mass market for encryption became more liberalized around the turn of the

---

[2]   Mailyn Fidler, Anarchy or Regulation: Controlling the Global Trade of Zero-Day Vulnerabilities 84 (May 2014), Stanford Digital Repository, *available at*: http://purl.stanford.edu/zs241cm 7504.

[3]   Andrea M. Matwyshyn, *Hacking Speech: Informational Speech and the First Amendment*, 107 NW. U. L. REV. 795, 809–10 (2013).

century. By 2002, the barrier for encryption exports was much lower, in an apparent victory for industry.

Established international law already includes treaties concerning dual-use goods, such as the Biological Weapons Convention (BWC). The BWC represents an attempt to find a workable compromise between the need for defensive and peaceful research into biological weapons, like developing a new anthrax vaccine, and the need to prohibit large scale research with ultimately destructive goals.

Like treaties, export controls can also be discussed collectively. One voluntary regime is the Wassenaar Arrangement on Export Controls for Conventional Arms and Dual-Use Goods and Technologies. The Wassenaar Arrangement is a multilateral export control regime that has 41 participating countries. In 2015, the Wassenaar Arrangement was amended to include "intrusion software" and products that are used in or interact with intrusion software.[4] The arrangement explicitly referenced "systems, equipment, and components therefor, specially designed or modified for the generation, command and control, or delivery of 'intrusion software'." The amendment was almost universally opposed within the computer security industry.

---

[4]   The Wassenaar Arrangement on Export Controls for Conventional Arms and Dual-Use Goods and Technologies, List of Dual-Use Goods and Technologies, *available at* https://www. wassenaar.org/app/uploads/2018/01/WA-DOC-17-PUB-006-Public-Docs-Vol.II-2017-List-of-DU-Goods-and-Technologies-and-Munitions-List.pdf.

Under the original wording, software becomes intrusion software under the Wassenaar Arrangement when it is "specially designed or modified to avoid detection by monitoring tools, or to defeat protective countermeasures, of a computer or network device." Specifically, the definition focused on software used for extracting or modifying data, or modifying the actions of a target program with external instructions, like with malware that takes advantage of a buffer overflow bug. Things excluded from this definition included hypervisors, debuggers, software reverse engineering tools, and digital rights management software. "Intrusion software" also did not include tracking software installed by manufacturers, administrators, or users.

In 2015, the Bureau of Industry and Security (BIS) at the Department of Commerce issued a proposed rule for implementing the Wassenaar Arrangement.[5] The proposal by BIS would have imposed license requirements for the export of technology relating to intrusion software. The proposed rule was not enacted, as regulators heeded the outcry from industry leaders.

In December 2017, the Wassenaar Arrangement was amended, with several changes that pleased the computer security industry. An important exemption was added for security researchers who are attempting to communicate vulnerability information internationally. Under the earlier

---

[5]   Department of Commerce, Wassenaar Arrangement 2013 Plenary Agreements Implementation: Intrusion and Surveillance Items, 80 Fed. Reg. 28853 (May 20, 2015).

wording, the Wassenaar Arrangement would have imposed burdensome licensing requirements on the researchers, making it more difficult to communicate time sensitive information. Still, the effects of the Wassenaar Arrangement will ultimately be determined by the countries that adopt it and how those countries interpret its terms.

II.   CYBER THREATS AND WAR

When it comes to applying principles of conflicts to battlefields, the Internet Age has created all new battlefields, and all new complications. The Internet is a game changer on numerous fronts. Though it began as a government project to ensure the resilience of communication capabilities in the face of disaster, the Internet has become a transformative technology that has dramatically morphed the way that people live, work, and play.

As of 2018, there is no formal consensus on the application of international law to cyberwar, but new research may help to bridge the gaps in understanding. The Tallinn Manual was first published in April 2013 and was the result of a three-year undertaking by a group of experts in international law and cyberwar issues. This undertaking produced a 300-page manual consisting of 95 rules, accompanied by explanatory comments, which provide a well-rounded and thorough depiction of the application of existing international law principles to cyber warfare. The Tallinn Manual is not a treaty like the ECC or a voluntary agreement like the Wassenaar Arrangement, but it has the potential to contribute significantly to the efforts of countries to understand and apply existing international law to the cyber realm. In 2017, Tallinn Manual 2.0 was released by the same workgroup. The new version of the Tallinn Manual expands on the legal analysis of cyber operations that fall below the "use of force" threshold of the United Nations Charter.

a.   CYBER THREAT PREPARATIONS

Some countries have sections of their militaries dedicated to cyber warfare capabilities. China's military includes "information warfare units," and North Korea's Unit 121 focuses on cyber warfare. Some recent estimates indicate that there are currently 140 nations that either have or are developing cyber warfare capabilities.[6]

The United States is one of the nations that have been developing cyber warfare capabilities. The U.S. Strategic Command ("STRATCOM") is the part of the Department of Defense ("DOD") that monitors attacks on DOD systems. The DOD is responsible for securing the .mil domain, and also operates the U.S. Cyber Command for conducting defensive and offensive computer network operations.

Cyber warfare activities likely will be considered "information operations" by the DOD. According to the Cyberspace & Information Operations Study

---

[6]   Susan W. Brenner & Leo L. Clarke, *Civilians in Cyberwarfare: Conscripts*, 43 VAND. J. TRANSNAT'L L. 1011, 1012 (2010).

Center affiliated with the United States Air Force, information operations are defined as including "electronic warfare, computer network operations, psychological operations, military deception, and operations security." Discussions of cyberwar will thus implicate all of the fundamental issues of war, such as how war is made and the rules that govern it, including the respective war-making powers of national leaders. As Brenner and Clarke note, cyber warfare is likely to be especially attractive to military leaders because it conserves human and non-human resources, though the low costs may also remove disincentives against offensive operations.[7]

Much of the emphasis on cyber operations is on the defensive use of such capabilities. United States leaders have publicly emphasized the importance of cybersecurity to national security. Analyzing and responding to cyber threats has long been an area of interest for the United States government. Operation Eligible Receiver was a 90-day cyber warfare exercise in 1997, in which 35 people acted as a rogue state. Reports from the operation indicated that both government and commercial sites were susceptible to attacks using "off-the-shelf" technology. In 2002, the U.S. Naval War College simulated a "digital Pearl Harbor" attack against critical infrastructure to gain insight into how such an attack would be carried out and what its effects would be. According to analysts, at that time an attack of sufficient strength to disable

---

[7]   *Id.* at 1013–14.

critical infrastructure would require over US$200 million on the part of the attacker.

Intrusion technology has developed a lot since 2002. Stuxnet demonstrated the potential for code to destroy equipment, and attacks on the Ukrainian power grid in the last few years show that malware can be used to create large scale disruptions. Many recent cyber incidents have been attributed to state actors. In 2018, the Director of National Intelligence, Dan Coats, warned of the potential for a 9/11-like cyberattack on critical infrastructure. While there are many skeptics who question the scope of the actual potential impact of cyberattacks on critical infrastructure, this is clearly a new battlefield.

Many other nations are also taking steps to prepare for future cyber threats. China publicly acknowledged in 2011 the existence of a unit of the Chinese military focused on cybersecurity matters, but emphasized that this unit's focus was on defensive measures, not offensive measures. In May 2014, five Chinese military officials were indicted by the FBI for cyber espionage against the United States. In 2015, President Xi Jinping of China and President Barack Obama reached an agreement where the nations jointly pledged to not conduct or support the cyber-enabled theft of intellectual property from each other.

The official position of Russia, as expressed in a submission to the United Nations in 2000, is that States are obligated to refrain from the development and use of cyber offensive technologies.[8] The Doctrine of the Information Security of the Russian Federation, most recently amended in December 2016, emphasizes defense and says nothing about offensive capabilities of Russian information security forces except to address the ability to counter cyberattacks. The full scope of controversies concerning Russian information warfare, especially concerning the 2016 presidential election, is outside the scope of this nutshell.

b.   INTERNATIONAL CYBER THREATS IN ACTION

Reality has gone beyond simulations and policy platitudes. In April 2007, cyberattacks originating in Russia continued for weeks and crippled Estonian computer networks in the commercial and government sectors. In June 2007, cyberattacks that originated in China disabled 1,500 computers in the Pentagon in Washington, DC. In July 2008, cyberattackers attacked Georgia with coordinated cyberattacks, and armed conflict between Russia and Georgia erupted shortly thereafter. In 2009, a series of distributed denial of service (DDoS) attacks caused the shutdown of half of Kyrgyzstan's internet service providers. The above attacks have not been conclusively determined to have been State-sponsored, and it is still very difficult to accurately attribute cyber hostilities to the culpable party.

---

[8]   U.N. General Assembly A/55/140.

None of the incidents referenced above invoked the use of the term "cyber weapon" like Stuxnet. In 2010, security researchers discovered Stuxnet, which has been described as a sophisticated cyber weapon designed to infiltrate industrial control systems, specifically those associated with Iranian nuclear infrastructure. Some estimates indicate that Stuxnet resulted in the destruction of as many as a fifth of Iran's centrifuges that were being used for uranium enrichment. No one officially came forward to take credit for Stuxnet, but it is generally believed that Stuxnet was the fruit of cooperation between the United States and Israel. The nature, expansive scope, and ambiguity of origination associated with cyber operations, as seen in the real world application of these technologies, underscore the need for thorough treatment of these issues in the law.

Stuxnet was not the beginning of cyber hostilities, but it was clearly a turning point. The operations involving Stuxnet allegedly started in 2007, though they weren't discovered until 2010. Security professionals also suspect Stuxnet of being related to three other malware packages: Flame, Duqu, and Gauss.

Malicious cybersecurity activities in the following years can be placed in three broad categories: surveillance and leaks, disruption of computer services or data, and disruption of physical infrastructure. Stuxnet was significant because it was among the first confirmed successful cyberattacks where the injury was physical, not just digital. Duqu, Flame, and Gauss were primarily focused on information theft and surveillance.

There have been many attacks that researchers suspect were carried out or sponsored by nation states. First there is the Stuxnet family of malware. Then in 2014, the United States government accused North Korea of hacking Sony Pictures, allegedly in retribution for the upcoming comedy film The Interview, which was about a plot to assassinate North Korean leader Kim Jong Un. Hackers sponsored by the Chinese government are alleged to have been responsible for the hack of the U.S. Office of Personnel Management that was disclosed in 2015. Many security experts suspect that the Russian government was behind the cyberattacks that shut down sections of Ukraine's power grid in separate incidents in 2015 and 2016. Also in 2016, hackers working on behalf of the Russian government were alleged to have been responsible for hacks of the Democratic National Committee. In July 2018, the special prosecutor's investigation issued indictments for twelve Russian nationals alleged to have been involved in the DNC hack, as well as cyberattacks against election infrastructure.

It is generally believed that many governments develop malware. The United States in particular has been criticized for a practice of hoarding zero-day vulnerabilities for future use, instead of disclosing these vulnerabilities so they can be fixed. The National Security Agency (NSA), for example, is widely believed to have developed a large number of hacking tools using such vulnerabilities. We know about this because a group identified as the Shadow Brokers stole many of these tools from the NSA's own servers in 2016 and released dozens of tools on the Internet in April 2017. By June of 2017, some of these tools had already been repurposed into ransomware attacks. The now infamous WannaCry attack quickly spread across the world in late May, causing over a dozen hospitals in the United Kingdom to cease operations until they had access to their computers again. Another malware package referred to as NotPetya followed in WannaCry's footsteps, though it is unclear if they shared the same NSA-related origin. NotPetya posed as ransomware, but security professionals suspect that NotPetya was just intended to cause mayhem, as attempts to pay ransoms failed. Some experts have claimed that both WannaCry and NotPetya were created by Russian intelligence agencies.

Governments have also outsourced the production of malware. This can lead to the creation of government contractors who specialize in creating spyware. In 2015, an Italian company called the Hacking Team had their own systems hacked, and the attackers leaked large amounts of sensitive data. Among this sensitive data were revelations that clients of the Hacking Team included several agencies of the United States. Other Hacking Team clients, according to the leaks, included the governments of Kazakhstan, Saudi Arabia, Nigeria, and Sudan, among others.

c. GOVERNMENT AND THE PRIVATE
SECTOR IN CYBERSECURITY

The line between government and the private
sector on cyberwar matters is blurred. In some
situations, the government has delegated to private
companies the task of operating cyber technology for
the purpose of collecting and analyzing intelligence.
Additionally, a nation's critical infrastructure is a
very attractive target for terrorists and could also
potentially become a target during wartime. In the
United States, critical infrastructure is often owned
and operated by the private sector. The laws of war
prohibit the targeting of civilians and civilian objects
that do not participate in the conflict, but as the
Tallinn Manual notes in Rule 39, this prohibition
does not apply if the object is dual-use—that is, used
for both civilian and military purposes. Because such
an object is used for military purposes, it becomes a
valid military objective. According to Rule 51 of the
Tallinn Manual, as long as an attack has a valid
military objective, collateral damage would be
permitted as long as the collateral damage is not
"excessive in relation to the concrete and direct
military advantage anticipated."[9] In other words, if
the United States finds itself at war with another
country, most of our information infrastructure is
probably a valid target.

Information infrastructure is a subset of critical
infrastructure. Critical infrastructure can be defined

---

[9]   Michael N. Schmitt, TALLINN MANUAL ON THE
INTERNATIONAL APPLICABLE TO CYBER WARFARE, Cambridge:
Cambridge University Press 159 (2013).

as systems that are essential to a state's well-being, including banking, communications, utilities, emergency services, and transportation. Most critical infrastructure is privately owned. A successful cyberattack could disrupt hospitals, defense systems, financial systems, and a variety of other important services. Cyberattacks against the transportation sector could result in airplane crashes or train collisions, while cyberattacks against water services could cause floodgates to open or result in untreated sewage being dumped into the local environment.

A key takeaway is that critical infrastructure is likely to be an attractive target during future cyber conflicts, but the private sector is largely responsible for protecting critical infrastructure. This overlap in the cyberwar context between civilian and military may prove problematic. International law currently provides protection to noncombatants, but it is unclear how these protections will apply on cyber battlefields. For example, should civilian-operated critical infrastructure be considered protected under international law such that it would not be a valid target during wartime? What degree of military reliance on critical infrastructure will be sufficient to render the infrastructure "dual-use"? Ultimately, the degree to which conventional war doctrines apply to cyberwar is not yet clear, though the Tallinn Manual provides very helpful guidance.

III. CYBERWAR ISSUES

Currently, there is a lot of uncertainty over how to address cyberattacks under international law and the laws of war. First, there is a substantial attribution problem because the origin of a cyberattack is likely to be unknown at first. Because cyberattacks are cheaper to undertake than physical attacks, cyberattacks may be conducted by more modestly funded groups. Attributing a cyberattack to a nation state will likely require a significant amount of information. Rule 8 of the Tallinn Manual emphasizes that routing a cyber operation through a State does not make the operation attributable to that State, and Rule 7 of the Tallinn Manual states that even if a cyber operation is mounted from governmental cyber infrastructure that alone is not enough to attribute the operation to that State.

Thus, if a cyberattack occurs, the first question concerns the identity of the attacker. If the foreign action is by a citizen and not by a government actor, enforcement of criminal laws against the perpetrator would be desirable. However, effective attribution of a cyberattack remains very difficult. In 2016, some major cyber incidents affecting the United States were traced to the Russian intelligence service GRU. A major source of this attribution is said to be the Dutch intelligence agency whose hackers had compromised GRU's systems prior to the attack.

The European Convention on Cybercrime provides some guidance and standards for addressing cybercrime issues. However, if a government is unable to identify a perpetrator, criminal prosecutions will be impossible. Even if the attack is attributed to a non-state actor and the host nation agrees to pursue criminal sanctions, some nations may punish the attacker differently depending on the identity of the victim, perhaps by increasing sanctions for attacking a more sensitive computer. Some areas of international law also address the investigative abilities of law enforcement, such as the Schengen Agreement of the European Union, which permits law enforcement officials to pursue suspects into another state, provided they cease their pursuit upon the other state's request.

If a cyberattack is attributed to a government actor, laws of war may apply, and this raises more complicated issues relating to cyber warfare. Cyber warfare operations could potentially limit collateral kinetic damage, but cyber warfare hostilities could nonetheless escalate into kinetic attacks. And as recent cyberattacks in the United States and around the world prove, the effects of cyberattacks can be severe. Consider, for example, ransomware attacks against hospitals that block doctors and nurses from accessing vital patient data, or power outages across wide regions of Ukraine.

There are many potential authorities to guide behavior in the cyber context. The Tallinn Manual, as discussed above, provides a good foundation for voluntary guidelines. There is ambiguity concerning how existing laws should apply to cyber conflict. Treaties are one source of international obligations, such as the U.N. Charter and the Hague and Geneva conventions. The International Telecommunications Convention, for example, was enacted in October of 1973 and prohibits parties from harmfully interfering with telecommunications, and the

Agreement on the Prevention of Dangerous Military Activities prohibits harmful interference with the command and control systems of military opponents.

Academic discourse often suggests that cyberattacks should be judged according to the Law of Armed Conflict ("LOAC") and the U.N. Charter. There are two central ethical principles of LOAC: first, if a state uses force against another state, it must have good reasons; second, if violent conflict erupts, parties should minimize unnecessary human suffering.

a. RESPONSIBILITY FOR ATTACKS

Case law has developed on some of the more ambiguous applications of these principles. Even if the national government is not directly in control of a cyberattack, the government may be held responsible for the acts of a third party within its borders. In *Corfu Channel*, the International Court of Justice ("ICJ") held that a state has an obligation to not knowingly let its territories be used for acts against the rights of other states, and this holding was reaffirmed in *Tehran*.[10]

In his article focusing on whether the actions of non-State actor cyberattackers can be imputed to the attackers' State of origin, Sklerov suggests the broadest standard for how much control a state must have over third parties: "indirect responsibility."

---

[10] Matthew J. Sklerov, *Solving the Dilemma of State Responses to Cyberattacks: A Justification for the Use of Active Defenses Against States Who Neglect Their Duty to Prevent*, 201 MIL. L. REV. 1, 12–13 (2009).

With the indirect responsibility standard, a state can be held responsible for the acts of a third party, such as a terrorist organization, if the State shelters the group and refuses to stop doing so after being asked by another State. This standard has been discussed in the context of the actions of terrorist organizations, including the response of the United States to the attacks of September 11, 2001. In that situation, the international community concluded that the actions of al Qaeda could be imputed to the Taliban government of Afghanistan. However, as Sklerov notes, any cross-border operations in response should be limited to targeting the non-state actor that executed the initial attack.

The "indirect responsibility" test focuses on the existence and breach of a duty held by the host state. Duties owed by a country under customary international law may include passing stringent laws criminalizing certain conduct, vigorously investigating crimes, prosecuting the attackers, and cooperating with the victim state during the investigation. There are also international law cases supporting the existence of an affirmative duty on the part of states to prevent attacks on other states. Whether these cases apply to cyberattacks as well as kinetic attacks, however, is an open question.

The "indirect responsibility" test could result in a finding that the host state has breached a duty that it owes to other states, but this breach of a duty does not necessarily mean that the victim state is now embroiled in international armed conflict with the host state. It could have many negative repercussions if hostilities by a non-state actor are interpreted as creating a situation of international armed conflict. Thus, the tests that evaluate whether hostilities by a non-state actor can be imputed to a state sufficient to declare that an international armed conflict exists are considerably narrower than the "indirect responsibility" test.

In note 2 accompanying Rule 22 of the Tallinn Manual, the experts adopted an "overall control" standard for determining when the actions of non-state actors can result in a finding that the conflict is of an international nature. In the cyber conflict context, a state would have to exercise overall control, beyond mere financial control, to have the actions of the non-state actor interpreted as being of an international nature. The "overall control" test is derived from the *Tadić* case decided before the International Criminal Court for the former Yugoslavia, where the focus was on whether a foreign state exercised "overall control" over an organized and hierarchically structured group. This "overall control" test requires that the foreign State also assist with the planning of the organization's military or paramilitary activity, but does not require that the foreign state actually give the orders that led to the non-state actors' violations of international law.

A third, still narrower option is the "effective control" test of the International Court of Justice in the *Nicaragua* case. Under the *Nicaragua* test, to show effective control, it must be established that the state "directed or enforced the perpetration of the acts contrary to human rights and humanitarian law alleged by the applicant State."[11] This test is narrower than the "overall control" test because it requires that the foreign state that supported the non-state actors must also have given the commands that resulted in actions that violated international law. In Rule 24, the Tallinn Manual adopts a variation of the effective control test to impose criminal liability on commanders for the actions of subordinates.[12]

b.   THE LAW OF WAR

If cyber hostilities can be imputed to a State, the Law of War will apply. There are two parts to the Law of War: *jus ad bellum*, which is the law of conflict management, and *jus in bello*, which is the law of armed conflict. *Jus ad bellum* is the body of law that applies prior to a conflict (such as Article 2(4) of the U.N. Charter, which prohibits uses of force), while *jus in bello* governs behavior during a conflict and is primarily governed by the Hague and Geneva conventions and customary international law.

It is unclear if *jus ad bellum* provides adequate safeguards to address cyberattacks, in part because of difficulties in attributing and characterizing cyberattacks. The Tallinn Manual emphasizes in Rule 10 that a cyberattack is unlawful under *jus ad*

---

[11]   Military and Paramilitary Activities in and against Nicaragua (Nicar. v. U.S.), 1986 I.C.J. 14, ¶ 115 (June 27).

[12]   Michael N. Schmitt, TALLINN MANUAL ON THE INTERNATIONAL APPLICABLE TO CYBER WARFARE, Cambridge: Cambridge University Press 91 (2013).

bellum if it constitutes a threat or use of force against a State.[13] Rule 11 of the Tallinn Manual states that a cyber operation should be considered a "use of force" if its scale and effects are similar to those of non-cyber operations that are a use of force.[14] The U.N. Charter is frequently cited in the context of international law and cyberattacks. The provisions of the U.N. Charter that are especially relevant to this discussion are Articles 2(4), 39, and 51.

Article 2(4) prohibits "the threat or use of force" against states in a "manner inconsistent with the Purposes of the United Nations." There are only two exceptions to this absolute prohibition on uses of force: acts authorized by the Security Council, and acts undertaken in self-defense. Article 39 gives the U.N. Security Council the authority to (1) determine when there exists a threat to or breach of the peace or an act of aggression and (2) to make recommendations to preserve international peace and security. Under Article 51, there is a right to use self-defense in response to an "armed attack" against a U.N. member, though the party utilizing self-defense must notify the Security Council. Article 42 permits the Security Council to use military force in order to restore peace when the conditions are met in Articles 39, 41, and 42.

---

[13]   *Id.* at 42.
[14]   *Id.* at 45.

c.   JUS AD BELLUM: USES OF FORCE AND ARMED ATTACKS

It is sometimes unclear what a "use of force" is under U.N. Charter Article 2(4). Generally, economic sanctions are not considered uses of force, but economic blockades are. Conventional weapon attacks definitely fall within the category of "use of force" in Article 2(4), and cyberattacks that are intended to cause physical damage or injury might also be categorized as uses of force. The international community is largely unsettled, however, on whether cyberattacks in general can be considered weapons, uses of force, or armed attacks. Rule 11 of the Tallinn Manual adopts a "scale and effects" test that would draw comparisons to non-cyber operations with comparable scale and effects when determining if a cyber operation is a use of force or an armed attack.[15]

However, before the scale and effects can be analyzed, there is a threshold issue, because the U.N. Charter does not define the terms "use of force" or "armed attack." Though the articles of the U.N. Charter do not contain clear-cut definitions of these terms, there are some additional documents that may provide guidance about how these terms should be understood.

According   to   the   official   commentary accompanying Common Article 2 of the Geneva Conventions, "de facto hostilities" are sufficient to find an "armed conflict," which makes clear that the Convention intended for the term "armed conflict" to

---

15   *Id.* at 45.

have a low threshold. The U.N. General Assembly's "Definition of Aggression" resolution, which was enacted in December of 1974, provides examples of State actions that qualify as acts of aggression. That resolution also defines aggression as the "use of armed force by a State against the sovereignty, territorial integrity, or political independence of another State, or in any other manner inconsistent with the Charter of the United Nations."

The Definition of Aggression may be understood as providing guidance for defining an "armed attack" under international law, though the Definition of Aggression primarily refers to "armed forces" and aggression. Helpfully, though, the Definition of Aggression resolution refers to "acts of aggression *and other uses of force* contrary to the Charter of the United nations," indicating that not all uses of force are acts of aggression, but that all acts of aggression are uses of force. Some uses of force, it can be concluded, would be more or less destructive than an act of aggression.

But is an act of aggression on the less severe or more severe side of a use of force? The language of Article 39 refers to the Security Council's authority over "any threat to the peace, breach of the peace, or act of aggression." This leads us to conclude that an act of aggression is a use of force that does not qualify as an armed attack, because Article 51 explicitly reserves to states the right to respond in self-defense to an "armed attack." So "use of force" is a spectrum, and on the less destructive end, there are acts of aggression. On the more destructive end, armed attacks. Taken together, this suggests that "use of force" under the U.N. Charter is akin to "armed conflict" under the Geneva Conventions, and that the term "armed attack" under Article 51 of the U.N. Charter should be read based on its relationship to an "act of aggression" according to the Definition of Aggression resolution. Under this view, "armed attacks" are aggravated "uses of force," and "acts of aggression" are less severe actions that nonetheless trigger the authority of the UN Security Council.

When evaluating whether an attack that is a "use of force" rises to the level of an "armed attack," one method is to use Pictet's test, which considers the scope, duration, and intensity of the attack. Jean Pictet was a Swiss jurist and the General Editor for the Geneva Conventions of 12 August 1949. When applying Pictet's test, there are three recent models. Instrument-based models look at whether the damage caused was of the kind that previously would have required a kinetic attack, such as shutting down a power grid. Effects-based models focus on the overall effect on the victim state, such as an information attack on financial institutions that causes significant damage to the economic well-being of the victim state. Finally, a strict liability model would consider any cyberattack directed at critical infrastructure to be an armed attack.

One of the most well-received effects-based models for approaching this issue is Schmitt's, which proposes an approach that focuses on consequences, taking into account six elements to determine whether a cyberattack is a use of force under international law: severity, immediacy, directness, invasiveness, measurability, and presumptive legitimacy.[16] Another option for determining whether an action is a "use of force" and/or an "armed attack" is a definitional approach that looks at (1) whether the cyber weapon was used "against the property or persons of a state" and (2) whether a foreign state knowingly allowed the cyberweapon to be used against the victim by an entity under the legal control of the state.

One of the first concerns raised about the terms "use of force" and "armed attack" is that perhaps cyberattacks will not meet the requirements for either because the target is a computer or network instead of a building, a vehicle, or a person.

Another difficulty of trying to regulate cyberattacks is that cyberattack capabilities could potentially become widely available to non-state actors, such as terrorist organizations that have no intention to adhere to any agreements between nations, and this might in turn reduce the willingness of states to be guided by the U.N. Charter in their responses to international cyberattacks. However, countries that have ratified or adopted the European Convention on Cybercrime may have sufficient controls in place to effectively address cybercrime within their borders. Thus, if the ECC is an effective method of addressing cybercrime, adoption of the ECC could reduce the need to hold

---

[16]   Michael N. Schmitt, *Computer Network Attack and the Use of Force in International Law: Thoughts on a Normative Framework*, 37 COLUM. J. TRANSNAT'L L. 885, 914–15 (1999).

states liable under international law for cybercrimes committed by citizens.

The ECC is currently the only international treaty that addresses cybercrime concerns explicitly, and it stresses the need to address cyberattacks through cooperation between law enforcement and other parts of the government. The ECC directs signatories of the Convention to adopt criminal laws against unauthorized access and interference with data and computer systems. The ECC also contains provisions recommending procedures and safeguards for signatories to adopt in their domestic law, and includes several articles mandating international cooperation between signatories. The ECC establishes minimum standards that signatories should adopt and apply as cybercrime statutes, calling on signatories to prohibit illegal access, illegal interception of non-public transmissions, data interference, system interference, and misuse of devices. The ECC separately addresses two types of damage: (1) damage to data and (2) damage to computer functioning. In addition to criminalizing cyberattacks, the ECC affirms that states have a duty to prevent non-state actors from using the state's territories to conduct cyberattacks against other states. However, many critics consider the ECC to be ineffective because of the potentially major players in the cyber realm who are not signatories.

Even if a cyberattack can be an "armed attack" under some circumstances, such that an action in self-defense would be justified under Article 51 of the U.N. Charter, the scope of actions in self-defense remains vague. A more detailed discussion of self-defense is presented in Section IV below.

d.   JUS IN BELLO

Once the conflict begins, *jus in bello* governs. *Jus in bello* is traditionally focused on kinetic weapons, but the International Court of Justice stated in its Nuclear Weapons Advisory Opinion that the law of armed conflict applies to "any use of force, regardless of the weapons employed." However, there is not an accepted definition for "weapon" under international law, so it is unclear whether cyber-weapons would be considered weapons when the issue concerns States embroiled in conflict. Thus, just as the application of *jus ad bellum* is unclear when cyber capabilities are used prior to a conflict, the application of *jus in bello* will likely be unclear when cyber capabilities are used during a conflict. Because of the complicated nature of issues relating to armed conflict, the bulk of the first edition of the Tallinn Manual from Rule 20 onward was dedicated to the law of cyber armed conflict.

Jus in bello includes restrictions on targets, limiting targets to entities that directly contribute to the enemy's war effort and that would produce a military advantage if damaged or destroyed. *Jus in bello* allows for direct attacks on combatants, but noncombatant civilians cannot be targeted unless they directly participate in the hostilities. Combatants are defined under Article 43(2) of the Geneva Convention as "members of the armed forces of a Party to a conflict" that "have the right to participate directly in hostilities." The United States currently takes the position that there are three categories of people in a war: lawful combatants, unlawful combatants, and civilians.

Jus in bello also requires that the attacks be proportionate to the military advantage gained, prohibits acts of perfidy, requires adherence to the principle of military necessity, and requires actors to make reasonable efforts to distinguish between military and civilian assets and personnel in executing attacks. We describe each of these requirements in turn.

First, proportionality requires that the damage caused be proportional to the military advantage gained through the attack. However, a lot of intelligence would be needed to predict possible collateral damage from a cyberattack, and it would be difficult to refute false claims of collateral damage from states looking to assert that a cyberattack was disproportionate and thus violated LOAC.

Second, the rule against perfidy basically means that a combatant cannot use his enemy's adherence to LOAC against him through deceptive means. For example, it would violate the rule against perfidy for a combatant to use the emblem of a protected entity that the enemy could not lawfully attack, like the International Red Cross, in order to get close enough to execute its own attack. It is unclear if or when this principle might be implicated by an attacker's phishing activity.

Finally, the principle of distinction emphasizes the need to distinguish between military and non-military targets. The principle of distinction does not create an overt ban on indiscriminate weapons, but parties to a conflict are encouraged to use weapons that discriminate between military and civilian assets.

Another important aspect to *jus in bello* is the immunity from attacks enjoyed by neutral nations so long as they remain neutral, which is potentially complicated in the case of cyberattacks by the lack of national borders in cyberspace.[17] For example, Kastenberg expressed concern about whether a nation's neutrality in a conflict might be compromised if private actors of the neutral nation take steps to help government actors of a nation involved in a conflict, such as by providing support to computer systems that are under siege. Because of the important issues relating to neutrality, Chapter 7 of the Tallinn Manual is devoted to rules concerning neutrality and cyberwar.

Much of the discussion on the topic of cyberwar assumes that military doctrine on cyberattacks will adhere to the principles of *jus in bello*. The U.S. military is said to apply the standard principles of *jus in bello* to cyberattacks, taking the position that cyberattacks should meet the *jus in bello* requirements of military necessity, proportionality, and distinction. The U.S. Congress's National

---

[17]   Joshua E. Kastenberg, *Non-Intervention and Neutrality in Cyberspace: An Emerging Principle in the National Practice of International Law*, 64 A.F. L. REV 43, 47 (2009).

Defense Authorization Act of 2012 also explicitly states in Section 954 that the same rules that govern kinetic conflict will apply to cyber conflict. However, just as it is unclear how the principles of *jus ad bellum* will apply to cyber aggressions before a formal conflict has begun, it is also unclear how the principles of *jus in bello* will apply to cyber aggressions during formal conflict. The availability of new resources such as the Tallinn Manual is thus very significant. It is clear that cyberwar issues are viewed with growing concern on the international stage, and the Tallinn Manual is likely to just be the first of many projects exemplifying international collaboration in the interest of reaching consensus about these critical topics.

IV. CYBER DEFENSE UNDER INTERNATIONAL LAW

A number of international law provisions address issues of self-defense. Self-defense under U.N. Charter Article 51, anticipatory self-defense under customary international law, and reprisals are three possible doctrines for analyzing cyber defense. Oppenheim's treatise on international law asserts that a use of armed force can be self-defense when it is in response to an armed attack or, in the case of anticipatory self-defense, when (1) an armed attack is immediately threatened, (2) an urgent necessity exists for defensive action, (3) there is no practicable alternative but to act in self-defense, and (4) the action taken in self-defense is limited to the needs of defense.[18] The presence of a right of self-defense may also increase the deterrent effect of international law for the purpose of deterring cyberattacks.

Whether a state is privileged to act in self-defense in response to a cyberattack is governed by Article 51 of the U.N. Charter. This turns on whether the initial cyberattack is an "armed attack." The language of Article 51 refers to "the inherent right of individual or collective self-defense" in the event that an armed attack occurs against a U.N. Member. But it is currently unclear who should be given the power to determine whether a cyberattack is severe enough to justify self-defense under Article 51. One theory is that system administrators will need to be entrusted with characterizing an intrusion and deciding if cyber counterstriking is appropriate, in part because senior policy officials would not be able to be involved at all levels of the decision.

Article 51 preserves an inherent right of self-defense in response to armed attack, but just as actions governed by *jus in bello* are required to abide by principles such as distinction and proportionality, the use of self-defense is limited in turn by requirements for necessity and proportionality. Evaluating whether the necessity requirement is met involves determining whether a more peaceful resolution would be possible, evaluating the nature of the aggression and each party's objectives, and estimating the likelihood that intervention would be effective. Proportionality requires the response to be

---

[18]   1 OPPENHEIM'S INTERNATIONAL LAW 422 (Robert Jennings & Arthur Watts eds. 9th ed. 1992).

limited to the amount of force that is reasonably necessary to interrupt an ongoing attack or to deter future attacks, but this proportionality requirement does not require the response to be limited to the amount or type of force initially used by the attacker. However, Graham notes that the use of kinetic weapons to respond to cyberattacks might be disproportionate and less effective than responding in kind.[19]

In addition to necessity and proportionality, self-defense under *jus ad bellum* also requires immediacy, but the principle of immediacy is very broad under international law and could permit a response to occur days or weeks after the initial attack.

Cyber counterstrikes would be limited by these three principles and could not amount to retaliatory or punitive actions. As a matter of international law, therefore, it is essential that execution of cyber counterstrikes strictly adheres to principles of mitigation and not take on retributive goals. These requirements also echo the traditional requirements for valid counterstrikes under the "just war" doctrine. The just war doctrine for valid counterstrikes requires that: (1) there is a threat of grave damage in the absence of a counterstrike; (2) the counterstrike has a serious prospect of success; and (3) there are no practical or effective alternatives to counterstriking.

---

[19]   David E. Graham, *Cyber Threats and the Law of War*, 4 J. NAT'L SEC. L. & POL'Y 87, 98–99 (2010).

The "armed attack" distinction is central to the idea of self-defense under Article 51 of the U.N. Charter. Even if a cyberattack could be an "armed attack," it is unclear if a response in self-defense would be permitted if the attack is not attributable to state actors. In these situations, the victim state finds itself in a "response crisis," where they are unable to intervene in the other state's domestic affairs and must rely on the other state to address the attack through its criminal law system. However, in extreme situations, it may be recognized that a state has a right to respond to non-state actors in self-defense, such as in the case of al Qaeda attacks on the United States on September 11, 2001, in response to which the United Nations Security Council reaffirmed that the United States has the right to engage in self-defense under Article 51. It is possible that a nation may be held responsible if they have "indirect responsibility" for the actions of third parties, thus allowing a cyberattack victim to respond to a cyberattack by a non-state actor using self-defense. "Indirect responsibility" means that the state had neglected its duty to prevent persons within its borders from perpetrating crimes against other States. However, the victim state's targets must be limited to the non-state actor attacker unless their lawful cross-border operations are opposed with force by the host state.

The current international law paradigm thus limits the response options that are available, so it is difficult to respond to an attack without potentially violating international law. However, Sklerov suggests that responding to a cyberattack with a cyberattack is more likely to comply with the *jus in bello* principles of distinction, humanity, necessity, and proportionality than would the use of kinetic attacks in response to cyberattacks.[20]

Even when the source of the attack can be identified, the system administrator for the victim state's system must also map the attacking computer system in order to determine the system's functions and the consequences likely to result from shutting down the system. This would help ensure that active cyber defense complies with the principles of distinction and proportionality. Because of current technical limitations, it would likely be impossible to make a "surgical strike" against a specific attacker, and harm to innocent systems could potentially be viewed as violations of the Law of War's principles of distinction and proportionality. The danger of running afoul of international law is one reason using the most accurate technology in detecting, tracing, and responding to cyberattacks is of paramount importance.

Another debated issue is whether cyber counterstriking can only be undertaken by persons who would be considered "lawful combatants" under the Law of War. If a private party conducts a cyber counterstrike against a foreign attacker and causes harm to other citizens of that state, the private party

---

[20] Matthew J. Sklerov, *Solving the Dilemma of State Responses to Cyberattacks: A Justification for the Use of Active Defenses Against States Who Neglect Their Duty to Prevent*, 201 MIL. L. REV. 1, 79 (2009).

could potentially lose its status as a protected noncombatant.

International law also includes the concept of anticipatory self-defense, which is permitted when the need for self-defense is instant and overwhelming, there is no other way to respond, and there is no time for deliberation. This is the *Caroline* standard of anticipatory self-defense that arose following an attack on a ship in 1837. The immediacy requirement of anticipatory self-defense is relative to the strength of the state, and it requires that (1) the aggressor is committed to an armed attack and (2) the defender's ability to defend itself would be hindered if it waited to respond. If there is evidence of an ongoing campaign against a state, anticipatory self-defense may be authorized because future armed attacks are considered imminent.

It is currently unclear whether Article 51 of the U.N. Charter permits anticipatory self-defense. One argument is that, because of the language of Article 51, self-defense is strictly limited to responding to an "armed attack." An alternative argument holds that Article 51 merely codifies an inherent right of self-defense, and that anticipatory self-defense under the *Caroline* standard is still available as a response. But even if the *Caroline* standard applies, the requirements of the *Caroline* standard that the necessity for response be "instant, overwhelming, and leaving no choice of means, and no moment for deliberation" may make it more difficult for anticipatory self-defense to apply in a cyberattack context.

If self-defense is strictly limited to responding to an "armed attack," a lot of complications then arise due to the nature of cyberattacks, especially the fact that cyberattacks are very unlikely to be viewed as *per se* "armed attacks." Arguments about characterizing cyberattacks as armed attacks often look to the traits, consequences or effects of a specific cyberattack. As a practical matter, it would be difficult to argue that a nation is about to be hit by a cyber "armed attack" for the purpose of justifying anticipatory self-defense, when the determination of whether a cyberattack is an "armed attack" is primarily dependent on an analysis of the attack after it occurs.

Schmitt argues that anticipatory self-defense can be used to address cyberattacks if three factors are present: (1) the attack is part of an overall operation that culminates in an armed attack, (2) the attack is irrevocable as a step towards an imminent and unavoidable attack, and (3) the anticipatory response to the attack is undertaken at the last possible moment to counter the attack.[21] This arguably creates a high bar, however, and anticipatory self-defense might be largely unavailable as a justification for cyber counterstriking if Schmitt's proposed standard is adopted. The notes accompanying Rule 15 of the Tallinn Manual consider whether anticipatory self-defense might be an option in the case of an imminent cyber armed

---

[21]   Michael N. Schmitt, *Computer Network Attack and the Use of Force in International Law: Thoughts on a Normative Framework*, 37 COLUM. J. TRANSNAT'L L. 885, 932–33 (1999).

attack. Based on Note 4 of Rule 15, a majority of the experts involved in drafting the Tallinn Manual appear to support a "last feasible window of opportunity" standard, which would permit anticipatory self-defense "when the attacker is clearly committed to launching an armed attack and the victim State will lose its opportunity to effectively defend itself unless it acts."[22]

Another theory is that anticipatory self-defense may be authorized when evidence suggests an ongoing campaign against a state. Therefore, even if anticipatory self-defense may not be available before any harm occurred, anticipatory self-defense may be possible after an initial harm has occurred if there is evidence that the harm will be ongoing. In such a case, there would need to be evidence that a prior armed attack was part of an ongoing campaign and thus future cyber "armed attacks" of the type just experienced are "imminent."

In addition to the traditional concept of self-defense, states may also be entitled to use reprisals, or proportionate countermeasures, to respond to a use of force. Reprisals themselves, though, may not involve a "use of force."[23] Reprisals must also meet three additional requirements: (1) the countermeasure is used in a State-versus-State context, (2) the defending state told the aggressor state to stop, and (3) the countermeasure's effects are

---

[22]   Michael N. Schmitt, TALLINN MANUAL ON THE INTERNATIONAL APPLICABLE TO CYBER WARFARE, Cambridge: Cambridge University Press 63 (2013).

[23]   U.N. General Assembly Resolution 2625 (XXV).

commensurate with the harm suffered. Reprisals, therefore, are not an option if a state wishes to respond to an attack by a non-state actor. Additionally, reprisals would be unavailable as an option if cyberattacks are considered a "use of force" under international law. However, if the international community declares that cyberattacks are not a "use of force," and thus that a cyberattack thus does not violate Article 2(4) of the U.N. Charter, utilizing cyber counterstrikes in a manner consistent with the definition of reprisal would be a valid way for states to protect their interests in the event of a kinetic "use of force" by a foreign state. As noted, however, reprisals are potential responses to a "use of force" that cannot rise to the level of "use of force" themselves. If cyberattacks are not uses of force, a cyber counterstrike in response to a cyberattack would not be a reprisal. However, a cyber counterstrike to a non-cyberattack "use of force" that doesn't rise to the level of an "armed attack" would potentially be a way for a State to protect its interests without relying on the U.N. Security Council.

The discussion of reprisals in the Tallinn Manual uses the term "belligerent reprisals" to describe acts that are undertaken to induce the enemy's future compliance with the law of armed conflict.[24] The interpretations adopted in the Tallinn Manual suggest that reprisals can be uses of armed force, but the Manual also emphasizes in the text of Rule 46

---

[24] Michael N. Schmitt, TALLINN MANUAL ON THE INTERNATIONAL APPLICABLE TO CYBER WARFARE, Cambridge: Cambridge University Press 150 n.2 (2013).

that belligerent reprisals cannot target unlawful
targets.

CHAPTER 11
PRIVACY THEORY AND INVESTIGATIONS

I. PRIVACY AS THEORY

In the United States, the most important early work in privacy theory is generally considered to be Warren and Brandeis's 1890 article, The Right to Privacy. In the article, the duo famously characterizes privacy as the "right to be let alone."[1] The topic is said to have been suggested by Samuel Warren, though future Supreme Court Justice Louis Brandeis did much of the writing.

Samuel Warren had a special interest in the right to be let alone. In 1883, Warren married Mabel Bayard, whose father was a United States Senator from Delaware at the time. In 1885, Warren's father-in-law, Thomas Bayard, was appointed as Secretary of State under President Grover Cleveland. Warren was a pretty private person, and disliked the degree of interest that the press took in his family. Research of newspapers and gossip columns from that time period suggests that Warren's antipathy toward the press might have been agitated by the news coverage of the funerals of his sister-in-law and mother-in-law, and also by the public interest in his wife as she

---

[1]   Samuel D. Warren & Louis D. Brandeis, *The Right to Privacy*, 4 HARV. L. REV. 193, 196 (1890).

became close friends with President Cleveland's twenty-one year old bride.[2]

So Warren and Brandeis penned The Right to Privacy, in which the authors said that the right to be protected from publication of personal information is based on the principle of inviolate personality. The right was not unqualified. The authors emphasized that the publication of matters of the public interest would not be prevented by the right to privacy. This right would also not prevent the publication of private information in a privileged context like legal proceedings. The Right to Privacy was highly influential in the development of the common law of privacy, though courts did not always agree that privacy violations should be recognized under tort law.

The next major development in privacy theory came in 1960 with the publication of Prosser's *Privacy*. Prosser was a torts scholar by trade, and analyzed privacy harms in light of contemporary tort principles. Prosser's four torts, which are still the four main privacy torts in use by courts today, are intrusion upon seclusion, publication of private facts, false light, and appropriation. Modern privacy theory has on occasion developed in opposition to Prosser's formalistic approach to privacy, especially in the arena of information privacy, where injuries are difficult to quantify.

---

[2]   Amy Gajda, *What if Samuel D. Warren Hadn't Married a Senator's Daughter?: Uncovering the Press Coverage That Led to "A Right to Privacy,"* 2008 MICH. ST. L. REV. 35.

By examining privacy law, we hope to provide a useful analysis of how privacy theory has been operationalized. There are two major categories of privacy laws: those that focus on government investigations, and those that focus on data protection. The remainder of this chapter is dedicated to the privacy law of investigations, like the Fourth Amendment and the Electronic Communications Protection Act. In the following chapter, we explore privacy laws that emphasize data protection. This second category is where privacy laws are most likely to apply to the private sector in the United States.

II.   PRIVACY AS LAW—INVESTIGATIONS

With help from the insights provided by the Warren and Brandeis article, Prosser's privacy torts, and other scholars, the common law developed throughout the 20th century to acknowledge and remedy harms caused by privacy violations. Constitutional and statutory privacy law also developed during this time period.

As noted above, there are two main divisions of privacy law in the United States. The first division concerns the protection of the citizen from privacy violations by the government. These laws vary in their breadth, with a sliding scale between broad liability and broad defenses. The harder it is to show liability for a privacy violation, the stronger the defenses to the claim.

One recent legal change providing stronger defenses came in 2016 with the amendments to Rule

41 of the Rules of Criminal Procedure. These changes affect the process for obtaining a warrant. Specifically, the changes allow virtually any magistrate to issue a warrant for the remote access of electronic media when the actual jurisdiction "has been concealed through technological means." This transjurisdictional warrant authority also extends to investigations of violations of 18 U.S.C. § 1030(a)(5), which is the CFAA provision about unauthorized transmissions that cause damage, where the damaged computers "are located in five or more districts." This is generally understood to refer to botnets, giving authority to investigators to obtain warrants for remote access to infected computers.

The two main sources of investigative limitations in the context of technology and information privacy are the Constitution and the Electronic Communications Privacy Act.

a.   CONSTITUTIONAL LAW

In 1965, the Supreme Court in Griswold v. Connecticut declared that there are penumbras of rights that emanate from the primary rights enumerated in the Constitution, including a right to privacy.[3] Griswold concerned a law in Connecticut that prohibited the use of contraception by anyone, including married couples.

The Griswold majority saw privacy in the penumbra of several amendments in the Bill of Rights. The First Amendment, for example, implies a

---

[3]   381 U.S. 479 (1965).

right of privacy against government intrusion as in the case of NAACP v. Alabama, which concerned whether the government could force an organization to disclose its members' names.[4] Likewise, the Third Amendment's purpose of protecting home owners from surrendering their home for the quartering of soldiers is fundamentally a protection of privacy. The Fourth Amendment and its protections against unreasonable searches and seizures are also grounded in privacy values, as is the Fifth Amendment's self-incrimination clause. The marital bed, the Griswold Court reasoned, is well within the "zone of privacy" protected by the Constitution. The prohibition on the use of contraception would likely be unenforceable without egregious invasions of privacy, so the Supreme Court held the Connecticut law to be unconstitutional.

For Fourth Amendment claims involving evidence in criminal cases, a key inquiry is whether there is a reasonable expectation of privacy, which has been the standard since Katz v. United States in 1967.[5] The third party doctrine creates an exception for Fourth Amendment protections when the suspect willingly disclosed information to a third party. In both Couch v. United States and United States v. Miller, the Supreme Court held that by disclosing financial records to an accountant or a financial

---

[4]   NAACP v. State of Alabama, 357 U.S. 449 (1958).

[5]   Katz v. United States, 389 U.S. 347, 360–61 (1967) (J. Harlan, concurring).

institution, a person no longer has a reasonable expectation of privacy in that information.[6]

When a third party is involved, sometimes another issue concerns private searches. If the third party discovered the illegal activity and reported it to law enforcement, the private search doctrine generally permits warrantless searches that do not exceed the scope of the original private search. United States v. Jacobsen concerned both private searches and the third party doctrine. Federal Express workers opened a package that was damaged in transit because company policy required examination of damaged packages to verify that the contents were not damaged. The package contained bags of white powder, which DEA agents confirmed was cocaine. The Supreme Court said that a warrantless search cannot exceed the scope of the private search that revealed the contraband, but that any infringement of privacy caused by identification of the powder was de minimis.[7]

The Fourth Amendment is a recurring player in discussions of the constitutionality of methods of collecting digital evidence. In City of Ontario v. Quon, the Supreme Court *assumed*, but did not conclusively *determine*, that text messages obtained from a service provider would be protected by the Fourth

---

[6]   Couch v. United States, 409 U.S. 322 (1973) (finding no reasonable expectation of privacy in financial records turned over to an accountant for tax return purposes); United States v. Miller, 425 U.S. 435 (1976) (finding no reasonable expectation of privacy in financial records disclosed to a financial institution in the ordinary course of business).

[7]   United States v. Jacobsen, 466 U.S. 109 (1984).

Amendment.[8] The application of the third party doctrine to digital evidence underscores the need for clarification in the law, especially considering the technological savviness of many judges. During the oral arguments in *Quon*, Justice Roberts indicated confusion about how electronic messaging works, and expressed his initial thought that the Fourth Amendment would not apply if such messages were handled by a third party during transit.[9] Invalidating Fourth Amendment protections on the grounds that a third party has to transmit the data from one device to another would not leave many electronic communication devices protected, except maybe walkie talkies.

Next, in United States v. Jones, the Supreme Court considered whether law enforcement actors violated the Fourth Amendment by attaching a GPS device to a suspect's automobile.[10] The *Jones* case could have had implications for the current debate about a reasonable expectation of privacy online. However, though the majority in *Jones* concluded that the placement of a GPS device on a car violated the Fourth Amendment, this conclusion was based on

---

[8]   560 U.S. 746 (2010).

[9]   Transcript of Oral Arguments at 48–50, City of Ontario v. Quon, 560 U.S. 746 (2010) (No. 08-1332), *available at* https://web. archive.org/web/20130423001536/http://www.supremecourt.gov/ oral_arguments/argument_transcripts/08-1332.pdf (exemplifying the confusion of Justices Roberts and Scalia as to how wireless communications are transmitted).

[10]   560 U.S. 400 (2012).

a theory of trespass rather than on a reasonable expectation of privacy.[11]

The Supreme Court started to be more in favor of Fourth Amendment protection of digital evidence with Riley v. California in 2014. In Riley, the central question was whether a cell phone could be subject to a warrantless search incident to arrest. Riley's cell phone was a smart phone, and the Court acknowledged that smart phones were really pocket-sized computers that "could just as easily be called cameras, video players, rolodexes, calendars, tape recorders, libraries, diaries, albums, televisions, maps, or newspapers." The Court held that a warrant would generally be required before a suspect's cell phone could be searched, including in the context of a search incident to arrest.[12] Thus, the usual search incident exception for the warrant requirement did not extend police authority to conduct warrantless searches of cell phone contents.

Digital privacy is also central to Carpenter v. United States, a Supreme Court case argued in November 2017. But where *Riley* concerned the content stored on a cell phone, *Carpenter* is about metadata. The central question in *Carpenter* is whether a warrant should be required before investigators can collect historical cell site location data. In June 2018, the Supreme Court concluded that the collection of this location information was a

---

[11]   *Id.*

[12]   Riley v. California, 134 S. Ct. 2473 (2014) (holding that a cell phone's contents could not be searched without a warrant as part of a search incident to arrest).

Fourth Amendment search, and thus a warrant is required before law enforcement can compel the production of this information.[13] The Supreme Court further held that the third party doctrine does not apply to historical cell site location data. Writing for the majority, Chief Justice Roberts concluded that asking for this location information is not, as the government had contended, merely "a garden-variety request for information from a third-party witness."

The Carpenter majority further points out that the third party doctrine only reduces the expectation of privacy; it does not eliminate it. The Court reasoned that even in third party doctrine cases, Fourth Amendment protection may still exist for information of a particular nature. Writing for the majority, Justice Roberts said "There is a world of difference between the limited types of personal information addressed in [third party doctrine cases] and the exhaustive chronicle of location information casually collected by wireless carriers today." The majority also ruled that the enhanced subpoena process in the Stored Communications Act could not be used to obtain historical cell site location data, an aspect discussed below.

The decision in Carpenter is fairly narrow and is very much tied to the presence of physical objects. Under Carpenter, there is Fourth Amendment protection for this kind of automatically generated information that tracks locations for a particular communications device. Previous cases about

---

[13]   Carpenter v. United States, 138 S. Ct. 2206 (2018).

location privacy under the Fourth Amendment have concerned beepers in barrels and GPS devices on cars. Cell site data is more far-reaching because in many situations, cell phones are practically an extension of the body. The court points out that most people keep their smart phones within a few feet of themselves at all times.

The majority in Carpenter also cautions against allowing the "progress of science" to erode Fourth Amendment protections, quoting Brandeis's dissent in Olmstead v. United States. In this dissent, Brandeis cautioned against the use of subtler means of invading privacy without ensuring adequate Fourth Amendment protections. Olmstead itself concerned the application of the Fourth Amendment to phone wiretaps.

Cell phones have become ubiquitous in society. In the 1990s, trivia games were still a challenge, because verifying a lot of that information would require a trip to the library. Sitcoms could make entire episodes with a running gag about one character asserting an obscure statement of fact that the rest of the characters spend the next 22 minutes trying to prove wrong. Average households bought their own encyclopedia sets so that they could look up general bits of knowledge. In 2018, it seems like almost everyone carries around a device that allows them to tap into the whole of human knowledge in a matter of seconds.

In order to facilitate the quick transfer of information and communications, cellular service providers direct signals from cell tower to cell tower in order to transmit data between devices. That information about the data's path is then stored, including which cell tower was the final stop before the transmission to the device. In the early stages of the technology, this data was only effective for giving a general area where a device was located at the time of the transmission, but cell site data has gradually gotten more accurate. The transfer of information to or from the device is necessary for these signals to identify a person's location, but with the popularity of push notifications and the necessity of software updates, many smart phone apps end up in frequent contact with outside servers. This means that access to these records can allow law enforcement to map a suspect's movements in an increasingly detailed manner over a long period of time. After Carpenter, the message to law enforcement officials who want access to this information is pretty clear: get a warrant.

b.   ELECTRONIC COMMUNICATIONS PRIVACY ACT

The Electronic Communications Privacy Act consists of three substantive sections: the Wiretap Act, the Pen Register Act, and the Stored Communications Act. In addition to being a privacy statute, the ECPA is also potentially relevant to victims of cybercrime, because the prohibitions contained in these statutes may limit options for recourse following a cyber event. A traceback, for instance, can help identify the source of an attack, but the SCA prohibits using unauthorized access of an electronic communications service to obtain stored communications. The criminal provision of the SCA thus creates an offense that is functionally identical to Section 1030(a)(2)(C) of the CFAA, but which applies only to the facilities that provide electronic communication services. The act of tracing an attack to its source in a sense doubles any injury that was caused by the hacker's digital trespass across other systems.

i. Wiretap Act

The Wiretap Act broadly prohibits the interception of communications, but provides a procedure for law enforcement to seek a wiretap. The Wiretap Act is often referred to as Title III. Section 2511 of the Wiretap Act presents a general prohibition on interception of electronic communications and the use of electronic communications that were intercepted illegally.

Section 2518 sets out the procedure that law enforcement must follow to intercept electronic communications. The required procedures under the Wiretap Act require a higher showing than either the Pen Register statute or the Stored Communications Act. For a wiretap, the entity seeking the order has to provide a statement identifying "the particular offense that has been, is being, or is about to be committed."

Section 2516 lists the federal offenses that can support a wiretap order. Notably, felony violations of Section 2511 of the Wiretap Act are eligible offenses for wiretap orders. Wiretaps also should not be the first investigative method attempted. Section

2518(1)(c) requires a statement about the use of other investigative procedures before resorting to a request for a wiretap. Entities must also generally set an end date for how long the interception will be maintained.

There is some overlap between the Wiretap Act and the Foreign Intelligence Surveillance Act (FISA). Section 704 of FISA, codified at 50 U.S.C. § 1804, provides the procedures required to obtain a court order for electronic surveillance. Similar to the Wiretap Act, Section 704 requires details like the expected duration of the surveillance and a statement that the information sought "cannot reasonably be obtained by normal investigative techniques." Section 704 also requires the applicant to provide a statement of proposed minimization procedures to minimize the collection of "information concerning unconsenting United States persons." Section 702 of FISA, codified at 50 U.S.C. § 1802, provides procedures by which the Attorney General can authorize surveillance without a warrant. Minimization procedures are still required for warrantless surveillance orders. Additionally, the Attorney General must certify under oath that there is "no substantial likelihood" of collecting communication contents where one of the parties is a United States person.

ii. Pen Registers

The Pen Register statute prohibits the use of pen registers without first obtaining a court order. The Pen Register court order requires a showing that the information likely to be obtained is relevant to an ongoing criminal investigation. Pen registers reveal the non-content aspects of the communication, like time, duration, phone numbers, or IP addresses. Service providers are explicitly excluded from the definition of pen register when they record this type of metadata in the ordinary course of business. Pen registers moreover generally obtain the real time metadata. There are significant modern controversies about the collection of stored metadata, which falls within the third part of the ECPA, the Stored Communications Act.

Which Part of ECPA Might Apply?

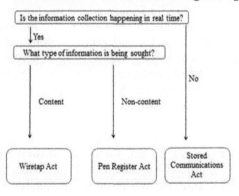

Figure 1: Different aspects of the ECPA

iii. Stored Communications Act

Wiretaps and pen registers were in use prior to the growth of the Internet. But as personal computers and the Internet became more common, the legal implications of stored data became more complicated.

The Stored Communications Act (SCA) was enacted in 1986 to address the growing gap between new technologies and Fourth Amendment protections.

Most of the language of the SCA has remained the same, but Internet technology has changed a lot since 1986. For example, consider webmail. The Internet works because computers on the network use identical protocols that enable interconnection so that data can be delivered across the network. One of the most well-known protocols is the Simple Mail Transfer Protocol (SMTP), which enabled email exchanges in the 1980s in the days before the world wide web. In the mid-1980s, when the SCA was enacted, the transfer of email was fairly fragmented. Email communications were transmitted from server to server and were stored at various locations temporarily during the trip before being downloaded by the recipient.

Today, webmail still may use the SMTP protocol, but it also uses the Internet Message Access Protocol (IMAP). IMAP allows emails to be accessed from anywhere with an Internet connection since the emails are perpetually stored on the provider's servers. The ability to access important communications from anywhere is important for mobility and mobile computing, but under the SCA as currently written, emails that have been previously read can be obtained by the government without meeting the high "probable cause" standard for a search warrant.

The SCA has three major substantive provisions: a criminal provision that prohibits the unauthorized collection of stored communications, another provision that imposes requirements on service providers for when they can voluntarily disclose stored communications under their control, and a provision on how government actors can compel the production of stored communications. Under the SCA, content and metadata are both considered stored communications.

The required procedures under the SCA vary with whether the provider is an electronic communications service or a remote computing service, the type of data sought, and in some cases, how old the data is. Emails that are unopened or less than 180 days old, for example, can only be obtained with a warrant. Past that, an intermediate order takes over, often called a 2703(d) order. This intermediate order is also sufficient for obtaining most stored metadata. A subpoena is sufficient for basic identifying information about subscribers. Courts were previously split on the issue of historical cell site location data, with some courts concluding that such information requires a warrant, and others concluding that location information is not protected by the Constitution. If the information is not constitutionally protected, that means that requiring a 2703(d) order created protections where previously there were none.

In the above section, we discussed Carpenter v. United States, which involves both the Fourth Amendment and the Stored Communications Act. Carpenter's argument stems in part from a warrantless search that was conducted using a

2703(d) order.[14] In Carpenter's case, investigators used the enhanced subpoena of 2703(d) to obtain 127 days of information about Carpenter's physical movements, consisting of 12,898 individual data points. The Court concluded that a 2703(d) order was not sufficient for the collection of historical cell site location data, and that investigators must show "probable cause" to obtain an order to conduct this kind of retroactive surveillance.

Carpenter did not invalidate the use of 2703(d) orders except as a replacement for a warrant for cell site data. To obtain a 2703(d) court order, the governmental entity must establish "specific and articulable facts" establishing "reasonable grounds" to believe that the information sought is "relevant and material to an ongoing criminal investigation."[15] This standard is less than the "probable cause" standard for obtaining a warrant, but greater than the standard for obtaining a subpoena. To obtain a subpoena, the government must show that the information sought is reasonably relevant to an ongoing investigation. The type of information sought also determines whether a 2703(d) order or subpoena must be accompanied by prior notice to the target. Additionally, the SCA permits notice to be delayed in certain circumstances, detailed in Section 2705.

The sufficiency of a 2703(d) order for stored emails was tested in the Sixth Circuit in United States v.

---

[14]   United States v. Carpenter, 819 F.3d 880 (6th Cir. 2016).

[15]   18 U.S.C. § 2703(d) (2006).

Warshak.[16] That case concerned fraudulent activity by the owners of the company that manufactured Enzyte, a heavily advertised nutritional supplement with commercials featuring the character "Smilin' Bob." Enzyte's popularity peaked in the mid-2000s. Warshak, however, did not market his products in good faith. Customers who had not consented to future charges were regularly signed up for an auto-shipping option, with their credit cards being billed at a regular interval.

The company also had a strained relationship with the merchant banks that processed credit cards on their behalf. These banks were not pleased when the rate of chargebacks got too high—that is, when too many refunds were being issued. To address this, the company routinely used methods to artificially lower the chargeback ratio for their sales, including a practice called double-dinging where a single charge was split into multiple charges, and an even shadier practice where employees made one dollar charges to Warshak's personal credit card up to his credit limit and then the company reimbursed Warshak for the charges.

The government had asked Warshak's information service provider (ISP) to preserve copies of Warshak's emails during the investigation, and compelled production of these emails with a subpoena under Section 2703(b) and also a 2703(d) order. The use of 2703(b) to compel emails indicates that the government characterized the ISP as a "remote

---

[16]   United States v. Warshak, 631 F.3d 266 (6th Cir. 2010).

computing service," which was significant because when communication contents are sought from an "electronic communication service," the SCA provides fewer alternatives to a warrant.

However, even with RCS providers, prior notice to the subscriber is required if the contents are being sought without a warrant. Warshak was not notified of the disclosure of his emails until a year later. While applying for the order, though, the government did seek and was granted a delay for the notification requirement under section 2705 of the SCA, but did not request further delays. The court acknowledged that this violated the SCA's notice requirement, but because the notice requirement was not violated when the emails were initially collected, it did not affect the legality of the initial data collection.

Ultimately, the Sixth Circuit ruled that the warrantless collection of emails violated the Fourth Amendment, but because the government displayed good faith reliance on specific interpretations of 2703(b) and 2703(d), the emails did not need to be excluded from trial.

The voluntary disclosure provisions of the SCA are also important to understand. For example, under the voluntary disclosure provisions of section 2702(c)(6), only communication contents are prohibited from being disclosed to non-government entities. It would not, therefore, violate the SCA if a cellular service provider voluntarily gave a suspicious spouse access to their partner's cell site location data. At any rate, most service providers probably have internal policies against such disclosures.

One of the frequently criticized aspects of the SCA is the distinction between ECS providers and RCS providers. This distinction is especially important in the context of voluntary disclosures under Section 2702(a). In Section 2702(a)(1), ECS providers are explicitly prohibited from disclosing to anyone the contents of communications that the provider holds in "electronic storage."

Section 2702(a)(2), however, prohibits RCS providers from disclosing communication contents, subject to two conditions. First, Section 2702(a)(2)(A) refers to data which is carried or maintained by the RCS service "on behalf of, and received by means of electronic transmission from . . . a subscriber or customer of such service."

Second, under Section 2702(a)(2)(B), the service provider is prohibited from disclosing communication contents carried or maintained "solely for the purpose of providing storage or computer processing services to such subscriber or customer, *if* the provider is not authorized to access the contents of any such communications for purposes of providing any services other than storage or computer processing." This phrase has often been applied by courts as if the second clause does not limit the first, which is arguably inconsistent with rules of statutory interpretation. What if a provider maintains communication contents for "the purpose of providing storage or computer processing services," but also has the authority under the user agreement to access the information for other purposes like, for example, scanning email contents to enable personalized advertising? Such marketing is often characterized as a service to consumers, but it is probably not related to storage or computer processing.

In 2018, Congress amended the Stored Communications Act with the passage of the Clarifying Lawful Overseas Use of Data Act, or the CLOUD Act. Prior to the CLOUD Act, it was unclear if the SCA permitted law enforcement to compel the production of data stored in a foreign country. In 2016, the Second Circuit relied on the presumption against extraterritoriality in quashing a warrant issued under the SCA. That decision was appealed to the Supreme Court as United States v. Microsoft. The *Microsoft* case arose because law enforcement served Microsoft with a warrant for the contents of a web-based e-mail account, but Microsoft refused to comply with parts of the warrant because the data being sought was stored in Ireland. The CLOUD Act adds Section 2713 to the SCA, which clarifies that even when data is stored in a foreign country, service providers must comply with orders to compel production under the SCA. This is the part of the CLOUD Act that ensures that law enforcement agencies in the United States can use a warrant signed by a U.S. judicial officer to access data stored in a foreign country. Less than a month after the passage of the CLOUD Act, United States v. Microsoft was dismissed as moot.

The second part of the CLOUD Act ensures that foreign governments will be able to compel the production of data stored in the United States. To do this, the CLOUD Act also amends another part of the ECPA, the Wiretap Act. The CLOUD Act adds Section 2523 to the Wiretap Act, creating a legal device called an executive agreement to simplify the process of cooperating with data requests across jurisdictional lines. Executive agreements can be entered into between federal officials and "qualifying foreign governments" that meet certain basic requirements for privacy protections and cybercrime laws. If an executive agreement exists with another country, and that country's government orders a company to disclose data stored in the United States, the company cannot refuse on the grounds that the disclosure would violate the domestic law of the United States.

Section 2523 emphasizes that orders from foreign governments must adhere to standards similar to those for issuing warrants in the United States. Such orders must have the purpose of preventing, detecting, investigating, or prosecuting "serious crime." Orders must provide a "specific identifier as the object of the order" and must also provide "a reasonable justification" for the order based on "articulable and credible facts, particularity, legality, and severity" of the conduct under investigation. Orders from foreign governments with executive agreements must be subject to judicial review or something similar by an independent authority. If the order concerns the interception of electronic data, Section 2523 imposes additional requirements similar to those under the Wiretap Act. Such orders must have a "fixed, limited duration," "may not last longer than is reasonably necessary to accomplish the approved purposes of the order," and are only available "if the same information could not reasonably be obtained by another less intrusive method."

CHAPTER 12

PRIVACY LAW AND DATA PROTECTION

I. PRIVACY AS LAW—DATA PROTECTIONS

As discussed previously, the first major category of privacy law concerns protection of citizens from the government. The second concerns protecting citizens from having their privacy violated by other citizens. There are specific statutes that restrict how private industry can behave with others' data, but these generally focus on limited data categories. For example, healthcare information, video rental histories, and education records all have specific protections under federal law. The Drivers' Privacy Protection Act restricts the disclosure of personal information from motor vehicle records. In the European Union, privacy law broadly protects against infringements by private parties as well as governments. In the United States, on the other hand, data protection laws are broadest for government actors, and otherwise tend to single out specific industries.

In a previous chapter, we noted that personally identifiable information (PII) is often central to state laws governing data breaches. Likewise, PII is central to federal privacy laws. State data breach laws usually define the term to require a combination of identifying information like a name or social security number along with other information that might be of a sensitive nature.

The Privacy Act of 1974 uses a definition similar to those adopted in state statutes. The Privacy Act does not use the term "personally identifiable information," but it does define "record" to mean "any ... information about an individual that is maintained by an agency, including ... education, financial transactions, medical history, and criminal or employment history" combined with identifying information like a name, identification number, or something else particular to the individual like a photo or fingerprint.[1]

Under Section 200.79 of Title 2 of the CFR, personally identifiable information is defined more abstractly as "information that can be used to distinguish or trace an individual's identity, either alone or when combined with other personal or identifying information that is linked or linkable to a specific individual."

a.   PRIVACY LAWS APPLICABLE TO GOVERNMENT RECORDS

In United States law, a common theme is that legislators are reluctant to impose regulatory requirements on private industry in the absence of market failure. This may be one reason for the current patchwork of privacy laws that apply to the private sector. When it comes to data held by the government, there are more limitations. For example, the Privacy Act of 1974 and the Federal Information Security Modernization Act (FISMA)

---

[1]   5 U.S.C. § 552a(a)(4).

both require the government to take steps to secure government computer systems.

The Privacy Act of 1974 protects records of identifiable individuals when those records are held by government agencies. The Privacy Act of 1974 requires agencies to have technical safeguards in place "to insure the security and confidentiality of records and to protect against any anticipated threats or hazards to their security or integrity which could result in substantial harm, embarrassment, inconvenience, or unfairness to any individual on whom information is maintained."[2]

The Federal Information Security Management Act was enacted in 2002 and required government agencies and contractors to adopt cybersecurity measures. It was replaced in 2014 by the Federal Information Security Modernization Act. Under Section 11331 of Title 40, the Director of the Office of Management and Budget is authorized to create binding information security standards based on standards proposed by the National Institute of Standards and Technology (NIST). NIST is empowered and required by law to develop such standards for use by government agencies under 15 U.S.C. § 278g–3. These standards are separate from the Cybersecurity Framework, which NIST developed as a voluntary information security standard for use by the private sector, especially private operators of critical infrastructure.

---

[2]   5 U.S.C. § 552a(e)(10).

As states developed more high tech methods of identifying citizens, laws have also developed to take these new capabilities into account. States are increasingly acknowledging and regulating the use of biometric data. Each state has set a legal definition of "biometric information." It is important to distinguish what types of data fall under the purview of each state's definition, as the scope and expansiveness of coverage may serve to include or exclude certain forms of biometric security.

In Illinois, the Biometric Information Protection Act (BIPA) defines "biometric identifiers" as "retina or iris scan, fingerprint, voiceprint, or scan of hand or face geometry." BIPA also applies to "biometric information," defined as "any information, regardless of how it is captured, converted, stored, or shared, based on an individual's biometric identifier used to identify an individual."[3] The additional coverage of "biometric information" means that any data transformations, such as reducing retina or fingerprint scans to mathematical functions, are themselves protected. BIPA, however, excludes writing samples, written signatures, photographs in general, human biological samples for scientific testing, demographic data, tattoo descriptions, physical descriptions such as height, weight, or eye color, or information captured from patients in a health care setting.

Texas only extends biometric data protection to biometric identifiers, which include "retina or iris

---

[3]   740 ILCS 14/10.

scan, fingerprint, voiceprint, or scan of hand or face geometry," broadly similar to BIPA standards. However, unlike BIPA, Texas does not include "biometric information" in its definition, meaning that abstract representations of biometric data, or analyses of biometric data, are themselves not protected under Texas law.[4]

In Washington, a biometric identifier is defined as "data generated by automatic measurements of an individual's biological characteristics," including "fingerprints, voiceprints, eye retinas, irises, or other unique biological patterns or characteristics that is used to identify a specific individual."[5] While broader and more expansive than Texas' definition, and even potentially broader than BIPA definitions, the law does not explicitly enumerate facial geometries or hand shapes. Further, Washington specifically excludes "physical or digital photograph, video or audio recording or data generated therefrom," suggesting that lawmakers have carved an exception with regards to facial recognition technologies. Washington's law includes any data generated as a consequence of analyzing biometric information, but carves out specific exceptions for certain industries, such as time-keeping applications for monitoring employee work schedules.

---

[4]   Tex. Bus. & Com. Code Ann. § 503.001(a).

[5]   Wash. Rev. Code § 19.375.010.

b.   PRIVACY LAWS TARGETING
THE PRIVATE SECTOR

The U.S. Code contains a patchwork of federal privacy laws aimed at protecting specific types of information, in contrast with the EU's broad approach to data privacy. The Health Insurance Portability and Accountability Act (HIPAA) is most widely known for the privacy statements that patients have to sign or initial seemingly every time they go to see a doctor. In addition to requirements aimed at protecting privacy, HIPAA also has information security rules. Among other things, covered entities are required to "protect against any reasonably anticipated threats or hazards to the security or integrity of [protected health information]."[6]

The biggest focus of HIPAA is on protecting medical information from unauthorized disclosures. Because such a large percentage of debt collection activities are for medical debt, Congress also amended the Fair Credit Reporting Act to prohibit consumer reporting agencies from disclosing medical information about consumers except in very limited circumstances. Such information can be released as part of an insurance transaction with the consumer's "affirmative consent," for employment purposes when the information is relevant and "the consumer provides specific written consent," and for the collection of medical debt provided that the information about the nature of the services is

---

[6]   45 C.F.R. § 164.306(a)(2) (2014).

reported using codes.[7] Medical research can sometimes be conducted without patient consent if the information is essential and obtaining consent would be impractical, as long as specific requirements are met. These requirements include: 1) the Institutional Review Board (IRB) has approved the research protocol and use of data, 2) disclosure of the data presents minimal risks, 3) the research will not affect the individual's privacy and welfare, 4) a plan is in place to protect against improper disclosure, and 5) the data will not be reused for other purposes without new authorization from the IRB.

HIPAA restricts the extent to which private health information can be transferred and disclosed. Organizations that count as "covered entities" under HIPAA must comply with the privacy and confidentiality procedures of the statute and also comply with related regulations promulgated by HHS.[8] Health plans, health care providers, and health care clearinghouses are considered "covered entities" under HIPAA.[9] The HITECH Act requires notification of data security breaches when protected health information is involved. There is no private right of action under HIPAA, but violators can be punished with civil and criminal penalties.

Covered entities also must comply with the strict rules on privacy and security promulgated by HHS. The Privacy Rule restricts disclosure of patient

---

[7]   15 U.S.C. § 1681(b)(g).

[8]   Standards for Privacy of Individually Identifiable Health Information, 65 Fed. Reg. 82,462.01 (Dec. 28, 2000).

[9]   45 C.F.R. § 160.102.

information except in certain circumstances, and in those circumstances, the covered entities must still limit the use of disclosure of the information to the minimum necessary amount.[10] The Security Rule includes provisions addressing the protection of electronically stored personal health information.[11] This includes ensuring that employees are properly trained in security measures and also encrypting all electronic communications involving personal health information.

Health information is also central to the federal Genetic Information and Nondiscrimination Act (GINA). Under GINA, health insurers may not use an individual's genetic information in making decisions about eligibility or premiums, nor can they require individuals to submit to genetic testing. Employers may not consider genetic information in employment decisions, and cannot request, require, or purchase genetic information about an employee or a member of their family.

The collection of genetic information by the government is often subject to different standards. Under section 40702 of Title 34 of the U.S. Code, law enforcement is authorized to collect DNA samples from individuals in custody and from individuals who are on supervised release, parole, or probation. The Attorney General is permitted to collect DNA samples from individuals in custody, and the government is required to collect DNA samples from

---

[10]   45 C.F.R. § 164.502(a)(1).

[11]   45 C.F.R. § 164.302.

individuals that have been convicted of a qualifying federal offense. If DNA collection is authorized and the subject refuses to cooperate with the collection order, that is a criminal offense and is punishable as a class A misdemeanor. Under Supreme Court precedent, DNA and other identifying features, like fingerprints, can be compelled without violating the Fifth Amendment's self-incrimination clause.[12]

Another type of sensitive information addressed by federal law is financial information. The Fair Credit Reporting Act is one source of protection for financial information, though FCRA primarily applies to consumer reporting agencies. The Gramm-Leach-Bliley Act (GLBA) is another financial privacy statute, and it applies to the more broadly defined "financial institutions." The GLBA requires financial institutions to adopt safeguards to protect customer information against "any anticipated threats or hazards to the security or integrity of such records."[13] The GLBA further requires covered entities to protect against access or use of customer records "which could result in substantial harm or inconvenience to any customer."[14] The GLBA further requires companies to send annual privacy notices to their customers.

Other privacy laws have emerged along with social and technological developments. The Cable Communications Policy Act was enacted in 1984 to

---

[12]   *E.g.*, Schmerber v. California, 384 U.S. 757 (1966).

[13]   15 U.S.C. § 6801(b)(2).

[14]   15 U.S.C. § 6801(b)(3).

address the privacy concerns of cable subscribers. Presumably, this was to fill in the potential gap between cable services and common carriers like phone companies. Under the Communications Act, common carriers have a duty to protect "customer proprietary network information," which includes information about how customers use their service.[15] The CCPA provided guidelines that were similar but more flexible to encompass the new cable services without declaring these services to be common carriers.

An aside is warranted about the relationship between the Communications Act and the Internet pertaining to the net neutrality debate. Net neutrality refers to the argument that providers of Internet services should not prioritize one type of traffic over another. Most of the discussions about net neutrality regulations concern the Federal Communications Commission (FCC) because of the FCC's authority over telecommunications services as granted by the Communications Act. Title 2 of the Communications Act applies to telecommunications services, like phone companies. These services face more stringent requirements than other services and are considered "common carriers." Among other things, Title 2 includes requirements for data privacy and nondiscrimination. These requirements would only apply to telecommunications services, however, and between approximately 2005 and 2015,

---

[15]   47 U.S.C. § 222(h)(1).

broadband internet was considered an "information service," not a telecommunications service.

"Information services" are defined by the Telecommunications Act of 1996 as "the offering of a capability for generating, acquiring, storing, transforming, processing, retrieving, utilizing, or making available information via telecommunications."[16] In 2002, the FCC designated cable internet as an "information service" instead of a "telecommunications service" (which would have made it subject to common carrier regulations of Title II of the Telecommunications Act), a designation which was upheld by the Supreme Court,[17] and later expanded to include DSL service.[18] In 2015, the FCC enacted a rule that recategorized broadband providers as common carriers.

In October 2016, the FCC adopted new privacy rules to govern part of the relationship between internet service providers and their customers. These rules made clear that ISPs were not permitted to sell subscriber data to advertisers. The FCC's Broadband Consumer Privacy Rules concern Section 222, titled "Privacy of Customer Information." Section 222 requires telecommunications carriers to protect their customers' information, and limits the situations

---

[16]   47 U.S.C. § 153(24) (2006).

[17]   National Cable and Telecommunications Association v. Brand X, 545 U.S. 967 (2005).

[18]   *Appropriate Framework for Broadband Access to the Internet over Wireline Facilities, Report and Order and Notice of Proposed Rulemaking*, 20 F.C.C.R. 14853, 14864 para. 15 (Aug. 2005).

where these carriers are allowed to share this information with others.

Like many things, these arguments often come back to money. Broadband providers want to compete with other Internet companies for advertising dollars. Google and Facebook are two of the companies that are the most successful at monetizing consumer information. ISPs have access to a lot more consumer data than other companies, so they could make a lot of money by selling information about you to advertisers. But ISPs are not just a website that you can choose to not visit. Many regions do not have much competition among broadband providers, making it much more difficult to vote with your feet if you do not like how the ISP uses your personal information.

Federal law allows Congress to block agency rules within a certain timeframe following their passage, and in March 2017, Congress did just that with a joint resolution disapproving the broadband privacy rules. Congress accomplished this using the Congressional Review Act, which allows Congress to undo the action of a regulatory agency within sixty legislative days. The FCC of the Trump administration also took additional steps to roll back the reclassification of broadband to re-deregulate broadband service providers. The effect of this is that the current FCC has stymied the previous administration's efforts to treat Internet service like a common carrier subject to those provisions of the Communications Act.

The preceding paragraphs focused on the type of information protected (or not protected) by federal privacy laws. There are also federal statutes that were enacted to protect specific groups, like children, students, and Supreme Court nominees. In 1998, Congress enacted the Children's Online Privacy Protection Act (COPPA), which imposed significant new requirements for websites that advertised to children under 13. Put another way, COPPA is why websites like Facebook have a minimum age of 13 listed in their terms of use, and also why your niece originally lied about her age to get a Facebook account until she decided that Instagram was better.

The Family Educational Rights and Privacy Act (FERPA) addresses information privacy in educational institutions, and thus protects student privacy.[19] FERPA was enacted in 1974 and applies to all levels of education that receive federal funding.[20] "Education records" under FERPA include a variety of information held by the school, not just grades. FERPA defines "education records" as including materials which "contain information directly related to a student" and which "are maintained by an educational agency or institution or by a person acting for such agency or institution."[21]

FERPA protects privacy in two ways: (1) by ensuring that students and/or their parents have access to the students' education records and are

---

[19]   20 U.S.C. § 1232g.

[20]   20 U.S.C. § 1232g.

[21]   20 U.S.C. § 1232g(a)(4)(A).

provided with a way to challenge the contents of the records,[22] and (2) by prohibiting the educational institution from sharing students' education records with other people unless an exception applies or consent is obtained.[23] For example, before a student turns 18, the parent has broad access to these records, but parents of students who are 18 or older can only obtain the student's education records without the student's consent if the student is considered to be the parent's dependent for tax purposes.[24] FERPA regulations also set forth more specific guidelines for when consent must be obtained prior to the disclosure of information contained in education records.[25]

As for the third group that we mentioned three paragraphs ago, no, there is no Supreme Court Nominee Privacy Protection Act. What we do have, though, is the Video Privacy Protection Act (VPPA), which was enacted following the failed nomination of Robert Bork to the Supreme Court. Robert Bork believed that there was no penumbra of privacy rights implied in the constitution, and thus privacy protections must be conferred by legislation.[26] A writer named Michael Dolan lived in the same neighborhood as Bork and asked their local video rental store for a list of the movies that Bork had

---

[22]   20 U.S.C. § 1232g(a)(1).

[23]   20 U.S.C. § 1232g(b).

[24]   20 U.S.C. § 1232g(b)(1)(H).

[25]   34 C.F.R. § 99.30.

[26]   Michael Dolan, *The Bork Tapes Saga*, FORT LAUDERDALE NEWS, https://web.archive.org/web/20071009145026/http://www.theamericanporch.com/bork3.htm.

rented. The list included mainstream movies like Ruthless People, The Man Who Knew Too Much, and A Day at the Races. It was clearly more of a symbolic point than a character assassination, and Michael Dolan was not actually against Bork's nomination. Still, the vulnerability had been exposed, and policymakers were quick to enact the VPPA to add video rentals to the category of information protected as private by statute. One interpretation of this is that the VPPA represents the squeaky wheel approach to federal legislation, though it could also indicate that a lot of politicians realized that their video rental records were more interesting than Bork's.

States also adopt their own privacy laws. As discussed in earlier chapters, all fifty states have laws concerning notification about data breaches, and many have additional requirements in their laws. For example, regulations in Massachusetts require detailed data security procedures to protect the personal information of commonwealth residents.[27] The regulations include requiring things like the encryption of personal information and the "reasonable monitoring of systems" to prevent "unauthorized use of or access to personal information." Minnesota has a merchant liability statute that holds breached company liable if the breach affected "access devices," which is defined as including credit and debit cards, in cases where the breach victim had improperly retained card data

---

[27]   201 Mass. Code Regs. § 17.04.

after the charge was authorized.[28] The Song-Beverly Act of California prohibits merchants from requiring customers to give personal information like their address, zip code, or phone number "as a condition to accepting the [customer's] credit card." Similar statutes are examined in Chapter 6's discussion of state data breach laws.

c.   PRIVACY IN THE EUROPEAN UNION

In the European Union, privacy is viewed as a fundamental right. The General Data Protection Regulation (GDPR) was approved by the European Parliament and the Council of the European Union in 2016 and went into effect on May 25, 2018. The GDPR replaces Data Protection Directive 95/46/EC, which was enacted in 1995. Because the GDPR is a regulation instead of a directive, the GDPR went into effect without requiring member states to pass enabling legislation. Some provisions of the GDPR expressly permit some variation within the laws of member states. For example, Article 23 of the GDPR addresses how member states may restrict some of the obligations and rights enumerated in the GDPR.

The GDPR includes 99 articles and 173 recitals. Most of the recitals offer commentary and examples to clarify various aspects of the articles. Eleven articles provide general information about the GDPR. Twelve articles concern the rights of data subjects, and twenty articles explore the obligations of controllers and processors. Seven articles address

---

[28]   Minn. Stat. Ann. § 325E.64.

transferring personal data to countries or organizations not bound by the GDPR. Eight articles elaborate on available remedies and potential penalties. The remaining articles are primarily about the administration of the GDPR.

The GDPR applies to the processing of personal data. "Processing" is defined broadly as "any operation or set of operations which is performed on personal data or on sets of personal data." The GDPR regulates the behavior of controllers and processors of personal data. Controllers are the people or entities that determine how personal data will be processed. Processors are third parties that process data on behalf of controllers.

"Personal data" under the GDPR encompasses a very broad variety of information. The person to whom the information refers is called a data subject under the GDPR. Personal data is data that can be used to directly or indirectly identify the data subject, and includes the usual suspects like name and identification numbers. Personal data under the GDPR also includes location data, online identifiers, and "factors subject to the physical, physiological, genetic, mental, economic, cultural, or social identity" of the data subject. Article 9 of the GDPR identifies special categories of personal data that cannot be processed unless an exception applies. These special categories include race or ethnic origin, political opinions, religious or philosophical beliefs, trade union membership, genetic and biometric data, health data, and data about the person's sex life or sexual orientation. Importantly, data subjects are not limited to a controller's customers. Employees of the controller are also data subjects protected by the GDPR.

Under Article 3, there are three ways that the activities of a controller of processor can fall under the authority of the GDPR. First, the GDPR applies to controllers and processors that are established in the European Union. Second, the GDPR applies to controllers and processors that handle the personal data of data subjects located in the European Union. The specific wording of Article 3(2) refers to data subjects "in the Union," so by its language, it is not limited to EU citizens and could conceivably apply to protect the personal data of Americans on vacation in Europe. Third, the GDPR applies in situations outside of the European Union if public international law recognizes that a member state's law applies. The recitals of the GDPR give the example of a diplomatic mission or consular post to demonstrate this third option.

Article 5 of the GDPR establishes some basic assurances for personal data. Such data must be processed lawfully, fairly, and transparently. Data collection must have specific, explicit, and legitimate purposes, collection should be limited only to personal data necessary for those purposes, and personal data must be processed in a manner compatible with those purposes. Controllers also have an obligation to ensure the accuracy, integrity, and confidentiality of personal data under their protection.

Article 12 of the GDPR requires controllers to inform data subjects of their rights under the GDPR. These rights are enumerated in the remainder of Chapter 3 of the GDPR. Data subjects have a right to be informed about the processing of their personal data (Articles 13–15), a right to correct their personal data (Article 16), a right to restrict or object to the processing of their personal data (Articles 18 and 21), a right to obtain their personal data in a machine readable format to allow data portability (Article 20), and a right to be forgotten (Article 17). The right to be forgotten requires controllers to have the ability to delete all of a data subject's personal data. Controllers are also required to notify any recipients of changes to personal data made pursuant to a subject's request (Article 19). Data subjects also have the right to have their personal data processed by a human instead of an automated system if the processing could potentially have "legal effects" on the data subject or otherwise significantly affect them (Article 22). The controller has one month to respond to requests from customers asserting their right under GDPR, and cannot charge the customer for this response except in limited circumstances.

There are several ways for processing to be lawful under Article 6 of the GDPR. First, processing is lawful if the data subject has given their consent. The GDPR, though, holds consent up to a higher standard than many Internet users are accustomed to. Article 3 requires that consent be "freely given, specific, informed, and unambiguous." Article 7 sets out several conditions for consent. The data controller must be able to show that the data subject gave consent. Data subjects also have the right to withdraw their consent at any time, and the GDPR requires that withdrawing consent must be as easy as giving consent. The GDPR uses an opt-in model for consent where an active choice must be made to consent to processing. If consent was a condition of using the service, the GDPR suggests that dynamic may sway a court against finding that consent was freely given. Article 8 requires controllers to obtain parental consent prior to processing the personal data of data subjects under 16 years old, though this provision also notes that a member state may choose to set a lower age for consent to be valid, but in any case a data subject's consent will not be valid if the data subject is younger than 13 years old.

Processing without adequate consent may potentially still be lawful under the GDPR. Lawful processing may occur when it is "necessary for the performance of a contract," to comply with a legal obligation, to protect the vital interests of others, or when the task involved is in the public interest. There is also a broader provision that refers to "legitimate interests" making processing lawful, but the GDPR warns that a data subject's rights might trump those legitimate interests.

Personal data subject to the GDPR can be transmitted to a country outside of the EU, provided conditions are met. Under Article 45, if the Commission has already decided that the receiving jurisdiction ensures an adequate level of protection for personal data, the transfer will not need special authorization. If there has been no such adequacy decision, Article 46 requires the controller or processor to provide appropriate safeguards for the transfer.

International data transfers have been an important consideration ever since the passage of Data Protection Directive 95/46/EC. Between 2000 and 2015, data transfers between the United States and Europe were made possible by the Safe Harbor Framework and the companies that adopted it. The European Court of Justice threw out Safe Harbor in October 2015, and since 2016, these transfers have been governed instead by the EU-US Privacy Shield. Presumably, the Privacy Shield will continue to be used as a tool to determine if the company's safeguards were sufficient for compliance with the GDPR.

To comply with the GDPR, companies that do business with European customers are often advised to conduct thorough audits of their systems to identify the paths that information takes and where it all ends up. The GDPR also requires security measures and for companies to have a data protection officer. In the event of a data breach, the controller must notify the supervisory authority (generally a government agency) within 72 hours of discovering the breach. Data subjects affected by the breach must be notified "without undue delay."

The GDPR creates a lot of guidelines that any business must comply with if some of their business transactions involve people in Europe. Article 79 establishes that data subjects have a right to sue controllers or processors for violations of their rights under the GDPR. Article 83 sets out conditions for administrative fines. The maximum fine available under the GDPR is 20 million EUR or 4% of the controller's global annual revenue. Failing to report a personal data breach can carry a fine of up to 10 million EUR or 2% of the controller's global annual revenue.

II.   PRIVACY AND SOCIAL MEDIA

Though the federal government has several sector-specific privacy laws, the information technology industry remains largely unregulated in the United States. This may change, as popular opinion toward privacy on social media services seems to be shifting away from a permissive attitude towards data collection. Instead, possible privacy violations on social media websites are often judged based on whether and to what extent these violations go against the terms of use for the website.

If you had a Facebook account in January of 2012, Facebook may have altered what you saw in your newsfeed to see if it affected your mood. In 2014, a team of researchers published a controversial study titled Experimental Evidence of Massive-Scale Emotional Contagion Through Social Networks. One of the three authors of this article was a Data Research Scientist at Facebook, which is how the researchers were able to have almost 700,000 unwitting test subjects.

Most Facebook users keep updated about their social network using Facebook's Newsfeed tool. To conduct this study, researchers manipulated the

Newsfeeds of test subjects to either show them more positive or negative posts from their Facebook friends. Researchers then monitored subjects' posts to see if the emotional content of the manipulated Newsfeed influenced the emotional content of the subjects' posts.

On the Internet, it is common for companies to experiment with their user interface to see whether a new design would be better at keeping the interest of its users. After all, on the Internet, clicks are money. When companies do this to aid in design decisions, this is called A/B testing. Many technology professionals have defended Facebook's experiment as being similar to A/B testing. But Facebook wasn't trying to determine which interface was better for business. Facebook was deliberately manipulating what users saw in order to experiment on its users' emotions.

Many ethical issues were raised by this Facebook study. In the published article, the authors explicitly state that because Facebook conducted the study, the participants were already subject to Facebook's Data Use Policy, and because they had agreed to that policy, they provided informed consent. But according to archived websites, Facebook's data use policy did not say that Facebook could use your data for research until May of 2012 at the earliest. This means that when Facebook conducted this experiment, even if accepting a privacy policy is the same thing as informed consent, those 689,003 users had not consented to this research when the data was collected in January of 2012.

Facebook has long had problematic policies concerning user privacy. In 2011, Facebook entered into a consent decree with the FTC that bars Facebook "from making misrepresentations about the privacy or security of consumers' personal information."[29] Following publication of the controversial mood study, the Electronic Privacy Information Center filed a complaint with the FTC to request an investigation, alleging in part that the conduct violated Facebook's earlier Consent Order. The FTC did not take action at the time.

Currently, Facebook's main approach to advertising uses various data points about users. The Washington Post reported in 2016 that Facebook tracks 98 different data points, drawn from a combination of information posted to Facebook, certain websites that you visit while logged in to Facebook, and information collected by data brokers like Experian, Acxiom, and Epsilon.[30] Facebook has also drawn criticism for permitting advertisers to exclude protected classes. In a potential violation of the Fair Housing Act, landlords who want to advertise through Facebook could make an active decision to exclude African Americans from the

---

[29] Press Release, Federal Trade Commission, Facebook Settles FTC Charges That It Deceived Consumers by Failing to Keep Privacy Promises (Nov. 29, 2011), https://www.ftc.gov/news-events/press-releases/2011/11/facebook-settles-ftc-charges-it-deceived-consumers-failing-keep.

[30] Caitlin Dewey, *98 Personal Data Points That Facebook Uses To Target Ads To You*, WASH. POST. (Aug. 19, 2016), https://www.washingtonpost.com/news/the-intersect/wp/2016/08/19/98-personal-data-points-that-facebook-uses-to-target-ads-to-you/?utm_term=.4383ffb20740.

audience for their ad.[31] This example shows the potential for hiding discrimination behind what seems like an impartial algorithm.

a.   FACEBOOK AND CAMBRIDGE ANALYTICA

Interest in Facebook's privacy practices was renewed in 2018 with the revelation that Cambridge Analytica had purchased information drawn from the profiles of as many as 87 million unique Facebook users. The data was allegedly used to develop psychographic profiles to help political campaigns target users with the most effective ads, which some believe may have influenced the 2016 presidential election. Facebook also allegedly sold ads to Russian operatives whose goal was to sow discord within the American electorate in advance of the 2016 election.

In 2010, Facebook made a change in its platform to allow third party app developers to have more access to Facebook users. Facebook prohibited third party app developers from selling user data to others, but these terms proved difficult to enforce. The third party apps would have to get a user's permission during the installation of the app, but once that permission was granted, they had access to the specified user data. For example, the FourSquare app was used for "checking in" at physical locations, and the user could send a single click and the app would post the user's location to their Facebook friends. To

---

[31]   Machine Bias, *Facebook (Still) Letting Housing Advertisers Exclude Users by Race,* PROPUBLICA (Nov. 21, 2017, 1:23 PM), https://www.propublica.org/article/facebook-advertising-discrimination-housing-race-sex-national-origin.

do this, the app would need access to the user's location, the authority to post on the user's behalf, and access to the user's "friends list" to identify friends who use the app. By default, a lot of these apps asked for a lot of access, but users had the ability to opt out of some of these requests. Opting out of data collection generally required unchecking boxes during the initial installation of the app.

In 2013, an academic researcher named Aleksandr Kogan created a third party app called This Is Your Digital Life. The app consisted of a personality test, and the default app permissions were extremely broad. 300,000 people installed the app. Some of the people who installed the app gave the app access to not only their friends list, but also their private messages. All told, the 300,000 installations allowed Kogan's app to access the Facebook profile information of 87 million users. Kogan allegedly downloaded all of the data he had access to, and then sold that data to interested parties, including Cambridge Analytica. Armed with detailed records, Cambridge Analytica created psychographic profiles of users, and those profiles were allegedly used to develop products to promote fake news stories and propaganda to influence elections and support specific political campaigns.

In summary, for several years, Facebook allowed third party app developers to request broad access to user data, and many apps requested more information than was strictly necessary for the app's purpose. Kogan took advantage of this design with This Is Your Digital Life and harvested information on 300,000 app installers and about 87 million of their closest friends. Kogan sold the data to Cambridge Analytica, which then allegedly used the data to help politicians get elected.

During hearings before Congress in 2018, Facebook founder Mark Zuckerberg noted several times that this chain of events would not be possible on Facebook's current platform because in 2014, Facebook significantly curbed the potential access of third party apps. In 2015, when they learned that Kogan had violated the terms of his agreement with Facebook, Zuckerberg asserts that Facebook demanded that both Kogan and Cambridge Analytica delete the misappropriated data from their systems. When asked if the company had disclosed this incident to the Federal Trade Commission pursuant to the consent decree of 2011, Zuckerberg told the Senate that Facebook had not notified the FTC because they considered it a "closed" issue.

The FTC apparently disagrees, and has initiated an investigation into whether Facebook violated the earlier Consent Order. The FTC's findings are not available at the time of this writing, but a violation of the Consent Order could result in a fine of $40,000 per privacy violation. If Facebook is fined, the FTC will have to decide whether to set a fine based on the number of individual incidents, the number of individuals affected, or some other metric.

b.   CONTRACTS ON SOCIAL NETWORKS

Terms of service agreements (TOS agreements) and privacy policies are contracts that practically every Internet user must accept for each website that she uses. TOS agreements set forth terms governing the relationship between a service provider and its customers. Generally, web-based services targeted at individual users are accompanied by non-negotiable TOS agreements that favor the service provider over the end user. Privacy policies often accompany TOS agreements, and by agreeing to a website's privacy policy, the user consents to the terms contained therein. These terms typically address what information will be collected and with whom that information will be shared. Privacy policies often also address data security issues, like the use of SSL encryption during data transmission.

Under the common law of contracts, forming a contract requires mutual assent. When a contract is not subject to negotiation and is offered by the more powerful party on a "take it or leave it" basis, the contract is often referred to as a contract of adhesion. Privacy policies and TOS agreements typically meet the definition for adhesion contracts. Such contracts are not automatically invalid, but they may be subject to greater scrutiny. If a court finds that the contract is unconscionable, it may be unenforceable.[32] It is currently unclear the extent to which TOS agreements and privacy policies will meet the GDPR's requirements for freely given informed consent.

---

[32]   Bragg v. Linden Research, Inc., 487 F. Supp. 2d 593, 605 (E.D. Pa. 2007); People v. Network Associates, Inc., 758 N.Y.S.2d 466 (N.Y. Sup. Ct. 2003).

Congress enacted the Consumer Review Fairness Act (CRFA) in 2016. The CRFA addresses an issue relating to clickwrap agreements like those commonly found on social media websites. Most people don't read the terms that they're accepting, which can be a problem if they have a dispute with the company that provided the product, because these unknown terms are now part of a binding contract. The CRFA specifically addresses form contracts that restrict customers' ability to post reviews.

In 2003, a court in New York ruled that popular anti-virus company McAfee could no longer use language in its form contracts that prohibited customers from publishing reviews or benchmark tests of the product without McAfee's permission. That ruling, however, only applied to one company in one jurisdiction. Since then, similar gag clauses have continued to show up. For example, the owner of a rental vacation home might sneak in a line giving the owner the right to keep the initial deposit in the event of an unflattering review. The CRFA renders void any provisions of a form contract that prohibits customers from posting reviews or that requires customers to transfer their intellectual property rights in a review to the company.

There are exceptions, of course. The prohibition doesn't affect a company's ability to take action if there has been defamation, or if the review is unrelated to the goods or services provided by the company, or if the review is clearly false or misleading. Reviews can also still be removed for abusive or inappropriate content, or if they include confidential or other sensitive information, like trade secrets or medical information.

The statutory language gives the Federal Trade Commission the authority to enforce the Consumer Review Fairness Act. State attorneys general and state consumer protection officers can also investigate and sue companies that include these prohibited terms in their form contracts.

Ultimately, the Consumer Review Fairness Act should protect customers from one method that has been used to silence honest criticism. However, SLAPPs are still a problem. SLAPP stands for strategic lawsuit against public participation. 28 states, plus DC, have anti-SLAPP laws. The Consumer Review Fairness Act fixes the problem of companies bullying critics into silence using gag clauses in form contracts, but it doesn't fix the whole problem. Still, some argue that anti-SLAPP laws make it harder for sincere plaintiffs to ask courts to fix real wrongs, and it is not clear how we should control for abuses of the legal system.

III. BIOMETRIC INFORMATION PRIVACY LAWS

Finally, we will focus on a growing subset of information protection laws: those concerning the privacy of biometric data. Perhaps one of the most salient advances in technology in recent years has been the introduction of widespread biometric security features. For consumers, products like Apple and Android smartphones, laptops, and "smart" security devices are now using fingerprints and facial scans to positively identify users. Commercially, many companies are starting to use fingerprint identification in order to cut down on timecard fraud among employees, and secure access to sensitive documents. Even companies like Six Flags Great America and Ticketmaster have begun to use biometric security on tickets, ensuring that only the ticket holder may enter their venues, and preventing individuals from sharing tickets or reselling tickets.

Biometrics is the science of using the physical properties inherent in the human body to identify individuals. Fingerprints, retinas, voice matching, and even a person's gait can all be uniquely identifying, and thus used to unlock various secure systems. Companies are keen to develop biometric security systems to increase security, and even create more convenient methods of verifying a person's identity.

The theory behind biometric security is simple. By utilizing inherent biological features that are unique to an individual, we effectively turn our own bodies into keys; always attached, primed, and unable to be easily replicated. By adding biometric security features, users are also spared from carrying physical keys or remembering passwords, both of which can be lost or stolen through user inattentiveness. Important to note however, is that biometric security does not specifically deal with the human genome; the sequence of one's DNA is considered a separate field from what modern biometrics is concerned with today.

The relative novelty of biometric security has led to a paucity of states adopting specific laws regarding biometric data privacy. Without state legislatures placing rules on biometric security, how free are corporate and private entities to collect and store biometric data? Can companies like Google, Apple, or Facebook collect and catalogue unique biometric identifiers like fingerprints with impunity? And for what purposes can these companies use biometric data? These issues are especially salient due to the *permanence* of biometric identifiers; we cannot easily change common biometric identifiers like fingerprints or retinas, unlike our credit card numbers or passwords. Biometric data cannot be changed or replaced if stolen, making biometric databases especially fruitful targets for data thieves.

Few state legislatures have enacted specific biometric data privacy laws. Only Illinois, Texas, and Washington have specific provisions concerning biometric data on the books. Illinois' Biometric Information Privacy Act[33] (BIPA) was enacted in 2008, and is considered the oldest, broadest, and most expansive data privacy law in the United States. Following the passage of BIPA, Texas followed suit with the Capture or Use of Biometric Identifier[34] (CUBI) in 2009. Most recently, Washington enacted a set of biometric security laws[35] in 2017. Each state has promulgated a slightly different policy, and has carved out what each state

---

[33]   740 ILCS 14/1.

[34]   Tex. Bus. & Com. Code Ann. § 503.001.

[35]   Wash. Rev. Code § 19.375.010.

legislature believes to be the appropriate balance between corporate interests and individual privacy rights.

Some states[36] have rolled biometric information into the definition of personal information, which are already governed by existing general privacy laws. There has been little movement at the federal level concerning biometric security, and only the Children's Online Privacy Protection Act[37] (COPPA) regulates the collection of biometric data specifically from minors (and only covering the collection of a minor's image or voice).

Despite some differences between Illinois, Texas, and Washington, all three state laws share the following common characteristics:

- Apply to private entities;

- Require private entities provide notice before biometric information is collected;

- Limit or prohibit the sale or disclosure of biometric data;

- Mandate protection standards and retention guidelines in relation to biometric data storage; and

- Require the eventual destruction of biometric data when it is no longer used for the initial purpose it was collected for.

---

[36]   DE, IA, MD, NE, NM, NY, NC, WI, IL, WY.

[37]   16 C.F.R. § 312.6.

a.   DEFINING BIOMETRIC DATA

Each of the three states with dedicated biometric data laws has a legal definition of "biometric information." It is important to distinguish what types of data fall under the purview of each state's definition, as the scope and expansiveness of coverage may serve to include or exclude certain forms of biometric security.

In Illinois, BIPA defines "biometric identifiers" as "retina or iris scan, fingerprint, voiceprint, or scan of hand or face geometry." BIPA also applies to "biometric information," defined as "any information, regardless of how it is captured, converted, stored, or shared, based on an individual's biometric identifier used to identify an individual."[38] The additional coverage of "biometric information" means that any data transformations, such as reducing retina or fingerprint scans to mathematical functions, are themselves protected. But "biometric identifier" excludes writing samples, written signatures, photographs in general, human biological samples for scientific testing, demographic data, tattoo descriptions, physical descriptions such as height, weight, or eye color, or information captured from patients in a health care setting.

Texas only extends biometric data protection to biometric identifiers, which include "retina or iris scan, fingerprint, voiceprint, or scan of hand or face geometry," broadly similar to BIPA standards. However, unlike BIPA, Texas does not include

---

[38]   740 ILCS 14/10.

"biometric information" in its definition, meaning that abstract representations of biometric data, or analyses of biometric data, are themselves not protected under Texas law.[39]

In Washington, a biometric identifier is defined as "data generated by automatic measurements of an individual's biological characteristics," including "fingerprints, voiceprints, eye retinas, irises, or other unique biological patterns or characteristics that is used to identify a specific individual."[40] While broader and more expansive than Texas' definition, and even potentially broader than BIPA definitions, the law does not explicitly enumerate facial geometries or hand shapes. Further, Washington specifically excludes "physical or digital photograph, video or audio recording or data generated therefrom," suggesting that lawmakers have carved an exception with regards to facial recognition technologies. Washington's law includes any data generated as a consequence of analyzing biometric information, but carves out specific exceptions for certain industries, such as time-keeping applications for monitoring employee work schedules. For context, it should be noted that Washington is home to the main Amazon headquarters, a company that has been innovating in the area of facial recognition technology. Amazon's facial recognition technology is increasingly used by law enforcement agencies.

---

[39]   Tex. Bus. & Com. Code Ann. § 503.001(a).

[40]   Wash. Rev. Code § 19.375.010.

b.   COMMERCIAL PURPOSES AND THE SCOPE OF PROTECTION

The use for which the biometric information is intended can determine the coverage of the law. Texas and Washington both limit their biometric data laws to actions with a commercial purpose. Texas does not define what makes a purpose "commercial" in nature for the purpose of biometric data.[41]

Washington defines a "commercial purpose" as "a purpose in furtherance of the sale or disclosure to a third party of a biometric identifier for the purpose of marketing of goods or services when such goods or services are unrelated to the initial transaction in which a person first gains possession of an individual's biometric identifier."[42] Washington's law expressly delineates between a "commercial purpose" and a "security purpose," which "prevent[s] shoplifting, fraud, or any other misappropriation or theft of a thing of value." The effect is that Washington law is limited in scope; applying only to transactions dealing with "third parties," and only to "commercial" transactions.

BIPA in Illinois has no similar commercial limitation language, and applies broadly to all non-governmental commercial and security screening transactions.[43]

---

[41]   Tex. Bus. & Com. Code Ann. § 503.001(b).

[42]   Wash. Rev. Code § 19.375.010.

[43]   740 ILCS 14/5(a).

c.   NOTICE AND CONSENT

One of the largest issues that biometric privacy laws seek to address is how corporations gather and obtain consent to store vast amounts of personally identifiable information. Further, all privacy laws require that notice be delivered to persons submitting their biometric data. However, what forms of notice are acceptable vary between states.

BIPA has several specific requirements for notices. Notice must state (1) "that a biometric identifier or biometric information is being collected or stored" and (2) "the specific purpose and length of term for which a biometric identifier or biometric information is being collected, stored, and used."[44] Further, notice and consent forms must be in writing, creating higher compliance burdens for companies. In addition, BIPA mandates that companies make available to employees a written policy that (1) establishes a retention schedule for the biometric data; and (2) explains how employees' biometric data will be destroyed.[45]

In contrast, Texas has no substantive requirements on notice or consent. Unlike BIPA, Texas notice requirements do not require that a specific term or purpose be disclosed by companies to the public.

Last, Washington mandates that no person may give up a biometric identifier without first providing

---

[44]   740 ILCS 14/15(b).

[45]   *Id.*

notice and obtaining consent, **or** by providing a mechanism "to prevent the subsequent use of the biometrics for a commercial purpose."[46] Like Texas, the requirements of Washington's law are not explicitly set, requiring that consent need only be "context-dependent," and "given through a procedure reasonably designed to be readily available to affected individuals."

d.   RIGHT OF ACTION

Only BIPA creates a private right of action when biometric privacy laws are breached. In Washington and Texas, only the State Attorneys General may commence a suit.[47] This unique feature of BIPA ensures that Illinois remains a significant, if not the sole source of case law concerning biometric security and data privacy in the United States.

The right of action in BIPA was affirmed by the Illinois Supreme Court in 2019.[48] The Rosenbach case involved the use of fingerprints for park admission. The court held that suits brought under BIPA do not need to show actual damages beyond the violation of the rights created under BIPA.

e.   DISCLOSURE AND SALE RESTRICTIONS

In general, all three state privacy laws restrict the disclosure of biometric information. In order for a company to legally disclose biometric data, an

---

[46]   Wash. Rev. Code § 19.375.020.

[47]   *See* Tex. Bus. & Com. Code Ann. § 503.001(d).

[48]   Rosenbach v. Six Flags Entertainment Corp., 2019 IL 123186 (Jan. 25, 2019).

individual must render consent, or the disclosure is required by law. Further, if a disclosure is mandated by a warrant or court order, a company may lawfully disclose biometric data. Last, all three states also allow disclosure in cases where disclosure is necessary to complete a financial transaction authorized by the individual.

In regards to the sale of biometric data, BIPA completely prohibits the sale, lease, or trade of biometric information.[49] However, both Washington and Texas' statutes allow for the sale of biometric data when disclosure requirements are met. Though Texas limits situations of sale or disclosure to three instances:

- To identify someone who has disappeared or died;

- As required by state law or to pursue a warrant; or

- To complete a financial transaction.[50]

Washington has also enumerated several exceptions concerning biometric data disclosure.[51] Disclosure is permitted in circumstances where:

- "necessary to provide a product or service subscribed to, requested, or expressly authorized by the individual";

---

[49]   740 ILCS 14/15(c).

[50]   Tex. Bus. & Com. Code Ann. § 503.001(c).

[51]   Wash. Rev. Code § 19.375.020.

- "made to a third party who contractually promises that the biometric identifier will not be further disclosed and will not be enrolled in a database for a commercial purpose inconsistent with the notice and consent" requirements; or

- "made to prepare for litigation or to respond to or participate in the judicial process."

f. DESTRUCTION AND RETENTION OF BIOMETRIC DATA

Regardless of the state, all three statutes set some limits for the period of time a company may validly retain and store biometric data.

In Illinois, businesses must delete biometric data "when the initial purpose for collecting or obtaining such identifiers or information has been satisfied or within three years of the individual's last interaction with the private entity, whichever occurs first,"[52] setting a maximum limit of three years a company may hold on to data no longer in use before Illinois law mandates biometric data deletion. Additionally, BIPA mandates that companies must make available and publicly disclose their retention policies.

In Washington, a business may retain biometric information for "no longer than is reasonably necessary"[53] to comply with a court order; protect against fraud, criminal activity, claims, security threats or liability; and provide the service for which

---

[52]   740 ILCS 14/15(a).

[53]   Wash. Rev. Code § 19.375.020.

the biometric data was originally intended for. Out of all three statutes, Washington's is the most broad and flexible, allowing corporations to retain data for longer periods.

Texas features a flexible standard like in Washington, while also setting a definite and quantifiable time limit for data deletion. In Texas, businesses must delete biometric data "within a reasonable time, but not later than the first anniversary of the date the purpose for collecting the identifier expires,"[54] setting a one year limit that Texas businesses may hold on to biometric data after the original use for the data expires.

g.   PENALTIES

BIPA statutorily authorizes minimum penalties ranging from $1,000 per negligent violation, to $5,000 per intentional violation.[55] For both negligent or intentional violations, BIPA also allows for actual damages to be used in lieu of the statutory minimums, and whichever value is greater is preferred. Furthermore, the winning party is entitled to attorney's fees. Illinois courts have interpreted each individual breach of biometric data to be a violation of BIPA.[56]

In one of the few instances where Texas law imposes harsher penalties than BIPA, Texas' statute

---

[54]   Tex. Bus. & Com. Code Ann. § 503.001(c)(3).

[55]   740 ILCS 14/20.

[56]   *See* Rosenbach v. Six Flags Entm't Corp., No. 2-17-0317, 2017 WL 6523910, at *3 (Ill. App. Ct. Dec. 21, 2017), appeal allowed, 98 N.E.3d 36 (Ill. 2018).

authorizes penalties of up to $25,000 per violation.[57] Lastly, Washington law mandates that any violation of its biometric privacy act can "carry a civil penalty of not more than five hundred thousand dollars."[58]

IV. PARTING THOUGHTS

In this chapter, we have explored privacy laws that focus on the protection of information from misuse. Currently, these issues are largely addressed by state law instead of federal law. This complicates practice in these areas, and the legal community would be benefited by standardization. In the meantime, it has become more necessary for lawyers to be fluent in technology. Data security is an ethical concern for practicing lawyers, and evidentiary issues are increasingly electronic. It is important for the profession to evolve purposefully to adjust to the new technological climate, as the legal profession is centered on information.

---

[57]   Tex. Bus. & Com. Code Ann. § 503.001(d).

[58]   Wash. Rev. Code § 19.86.140.

APPENDIX

CYBERSECURITY STATE LAWS

State	Statute Category	Citation
Alabama	Computer Crime	Ala. Code §§ 13A–8–110 to 13A–8–119
	Identity Theft	Ala. Code §§ 13A–8–190 to 13A–8–201
	Dealing in ID Documents	Ala. Code § 31–13–14
	Data Breaches	Ala. Code §§ 8–38–1 to 8–38–12
Alaska	Computer Crime	Alaska Stat. § 11.46.740
	Spyware	Alaska Stat. § 45.45.792
	Identity Theft	Alaska Stat. §§ 11.46.565 and 11.46.570
	Theft by Deception	Alaska Stat. § 11.46.180
	Data Breaches	Alaska Stat. §§ 45.48.010 to 45.48.090
Arizona	Computer Crime	Ariz. Rev. Stat. §§ 13–2316, 13–2316.01, 13–2316.02

Arizona	Spyware	Ariz. Rev. Stat. §§ 18–501 to 18–504
	Identity Theft	Ariz. Rev. Stat. §§ 13–2008 to 13–2010
	Data Breaches	Ariz. Rev. Stat. §§ 18–551 to 18–552
Arkansas	Computer Crime	Ark. Code §§ 5–41–101 to 5–41–206
	Spyware	Ark. Code §§ 4–111–101 to 4–111–105
	Identity Theft	Ark. Code §§ 5–37–227 to 5–37–229
	Data Breaches	Ark. Code §§ 4–110–101 to 4–110–108
California	Computer Crime	Cal. Penal Code §§ 502, 523
	Spyware	Cal. Bus. & Prof. Code §§ 22947 to 22947.6
	Identity Theft	Cal. Penal Code §§ 530.5 to 530.8
	Data Breaches	Cal. Civ. Code §§ 1798.80 to 1798.84

California	Data Breaches at Government Agencies	Cal. Civ. Code § 1798.29
	Medical Information	Cal. Health & Safety Code § 1280.15
Colorado	Computer Crime	Colo. Rev. Stat. §§ 18–5.5–101 to 18–5.5–102
	Email-Related Fraud	Colo. Rev. Stat. § 18–5–308
	Identity Theft	Colo. Rev. Stat. §§ 18–5–901 to 18–5–905
	Criminal Impersonation	Colo. Rev. Stat. § 18–5–113
	Data Breaches	Colo. Rev. Stat. § 6–1–716
	Data Breaches at Government Agencies	Colo. Rev. Stat. §§ 24–73–101 to 24–73–103
	Records Disposal	Colo. Rev. Stat. § 6–1–713
	Security Requirements	Colo. Rev. Stat. § 6–1–713.5
Connecticut	Computer Crime	Conn. Gen. Stat. §§ 53a–250 to 53a–262
	Terroristic Computer Crime	Conn. Gen. Stat. § 53a–301

Connecticut	Email-Related Fraud	Conn. Gen. Stat. § 53–454
	Identity Theft	Conn. Gen. Stat. §§ 53a–129a to 53a–129e
	Criminal Impersonation	Conn. Gen. Stat. § 53a–130
	Data Breaches	Conn. Gen. Stat. § 36a–701b
Delaware	Computer Crime	Del. Code Ann. tit. 11, §§ 931 to 941, 2738
	Email-Related Fraud	Del. Code Ann. tit. 11, § 937
	Identity Theft	Del. Code Ann. tit. 11, §§ 854 to 854A
	Possession of Tools for Theft	Del. Code Ann. tit. 11, § 828
	Criminal Impersonation	Del. Code Ann. tit. 11, § 907
	Data Breaches	Del. Code Ann. tit. 6, §§ 12B–101 to 12B–104
Florida	Computer Crime	Fla. Stat. §§ 815.01 to 815.07
	Computer Crime	Fla. Stat. §§ 668.801 to 668.805

Florida	Communication Interception	Fla. Stat. § 934.03
	Identity Theft	Fla. Stat. § 817.568
	False Personation	Fla. Stat. § 817.02
	Unlawful Possession of Personal Information	Fla. Stat. § 817.5685
	Identity Theft Tools	Fla. Stat. § 817.625
	Data Breaches	Fla. Stat. § 501.171
Georgia	Computer Crime	Ga. Code §§ 16–9–90 to 16–9–94
	Computer Security	Ga. Code §§ 16–9–150 to 16–9–157
	Identity Theft	Ga. Code §§ 16–9–120 to 16–9–132
	Data Breaches	Ga. Code §§ 10–1–910 to 10–1–915
Hawaii	Computer Crime	Hawaii Rev. Stat. §§ 708–890 to 708–895.7
	Identity Theft	Hawaii Rev. Stat. §§ 708–839.6 to 708–839.8

Hawaii	Unlawful Possession of Personal Information	Hawaii Rev. Stat. § 708–839.55
	Data Breaches	Hawaii Rev. Stat. §§ 487N–1 to 487N–7
Idaho	Computer Crime	Idaho Code §§ 18–2201, 18–2202
	Computer Crime Against Banks	Idaho Code § 26–1220
	Identity Theft	Idaho Code §§ 18–3126 and 3126A
	Data Breaches	Idaho Code §§ 28–51–104 to 28–51–107
Illinois	Computer Crime	Ill. Rev. Stat. ch. 720, §§ 5/17–50 to 5/17–55
	Phishing	Ill. Rev. Stat. ch. 740, §§ 7/1 to 7/15
	Identity Theft	Ill. Rev. Stat. ch. 720, §§ 5/16–30 to 5/16–37
	False Personation	Ill. Rev. Stat. ch. 720, § 5/17–2
	Data Breaches	Ill. Rev. Stat. ch. 815, §§ 530/5 to 530/50
Indiana	Computer Crime	Ind. Code § 35–43–1–8

Indiana	Computer Crime	Ind. Code § 35–43–2–3
	Spyware	Ind. Code § 24–4.8–2–2
	Identity Theft	Ind. Code § 35–43–5–3.5
	Synthetic Identity Theft	Ind. Code § 35–43–5–3.8
	Data Breaches	Ind. Code §§ 24–4.9–1–1 to 24–4.9–5–1
	Data Breaches at Government Agencies	Ind. Code §§ 4–1–11–1 to 4–1–11–10
Iowa	Computer Crime	Iowa Code § 716.6B
	Spyware	Iowa Code §§ 715.1 to 715.8
	Email-Related Offense	Iowa Code §§ 716A.1 to 716A.7
	Identity Theft	Iowa Code §§ 715A.8 to 715A.10
	Data Breaches	Iowa Code §§ 715C.1 to 715C.2
Kansas	Computer Crime	Kan. Stat. § 21–5839
	Identity Theft	Kan. Stat. §§ 21–6107 to 21–6108

Kansas	Dealing in ID Documents	Kan. Stat. § 21–5918
	Data Breaches	Kan. Stat. §§ 50–7a01 to 50–7a04
Kentucky	Computer Crime	Ky. Rev. Stat. §§ 434.840 to 434.860
	Phishing	Ky. Rev. Stat. § 434.697
	Identity Theft	Ky. Rev. Stat. §§ 514.160 to 514.170
	Financial Information Theft	Ky. Rev. Stat. §§ 434.870 to 434.876
	Data Breaches	Ky. Rev. Stat. §§ 365.720 to 365.734
Louisiana	Computer Crime	La. Rev. Stat. Ann. §§ 14:73.1 to 14:73.8
	Spyware	La. Rev. Stat. Ann. § 51:2008
	Email-Related Fraud	La. Rev. Stat. Ann. §§ 51:2021 to 2025
	Phishing	La. Rev. Stat. Ann. §§ 51:2031 to 51:2034
	Identity Theft	La. Rev. Stat. Ann. § 14:67.16

Louisiana	Fraudulent Identification Documents	La. Rev. Stat. Ann. § 14:70.7
	Online Impersonation	La. Rev. Stat. Ann. § 14:73.10
	Data Breaches	La. Rev. Stat. §§ 51:3071 to 51:3077
Maine	Computer Crime	Me. Rev. Stat. Ann. tit. 17–A, §§ 431 to 437
	Identity Theft	Me. Rev. Stat. Ann. tit. 17–A, § 905–A
	Reporting Identity Theft	Me. Rev. Stat. Ann. tit. 10, § 1350–B
	Data Breaches	Me. Rev. Stat. Ann. tit. 10, §§ 1346 to 1350–B
Maryland	Computer Crime	Md. Code, Crim. Law § 7–302
	Email-Related Offense	Md. Code, Crim. Law § 3–805.1
	Identity Theft	Md. Code, Crim. Law §§ 8–301 to 8–305
	Data Breaches	Md. Code, Com. Law §§ 14–3501 to 14–3508

Maryland	Data Breaches at Government Agencies	Md. Code, State Government, §§ 10–1301 to 10–1308
Massachusetts	Computer Crime	Mass. Gen. Laws Ann. ch. 266, § 120F
	Computer Crime	Mass. Gen. Laws Ann. ch. 266, § 33A
	Identity Theft	Mass. Gen. Laws Ann. ch. 266, § 37E
	Data Breaches	Mass. Gen. Laws 93H §§ 1 to 6
	Records Disposal	Mass. Gen. Laws 93I §§ 1 to 3
Michigan	Computer Crime	Mich. Comp. Laws §§ 752.791 to 752.797
	Use of Computer in Other Offenses	Mich. Comp. Laws § 750.145d
	Banned Devices	Mich. Comp. Laws § 750.411w
	Identity Theft	Mich. Comp. Laws §§ 445.61 to 445.79d
	Data Breaches	Mich. Comp. Laws § 445.72
Minnesota	Computer Crime	Minn. Stat. §§ 609.87 to 609.893

Minnesota	Identity Theft	Minn. Stat. § 609.527
	Data Breaches	Minn. Stat. § 325E.61
	Data Breaches at Government Agencies	Minn. Stat. § 13.055
	Breach of Payment Data	Minn. Stat. § 325E.64
Mississippi	Computer Crime	Miss. Code §§ 97–45–1 to 97–45–33
	Identity Theft	Miss. Code §§ 97–45–1 to 97–45–33
	Using Another's Identity to Obtain Goods	Miss. Code § 97–19–85
	Data Breaches	Miss. Code § 75–24–29
Missouri	Computer Crime	Mo. Rev. Stat. §§ 569.095 to 569.099
	Civil Action	Mo. Rev. Stat. § 537.525
	Identity Theft	Mo. Rev. Stat. § 570.223
	Trafficking Stolen Identities	Mo. Rev. Stat. § 570.224
	Using a Fraudulent Credit Device	Mo. Rev. Stat. § 570.130
	Identity Theft Incident Reports	Mo. Rev. Stat. § 595.232

Missouri	Data Breaches	Mo. Rev. Stat. § 407.1500
Montana	Computer Crime	Mont. Code Ann. §§ 45–6–310 to 311
	Phishing	Mont. Code Ann. § 30–14–1712
	Identity Theft	Mont. Code Ann. § 45–6–332
	Impersonation	Mont. Code Ann. § 45–8–220
	Identity Theft Reporting	Mont. Code Ann. §§ 46–24–218 to 46–24–220
	Data Breaches	Mont. Code Ann. § 30–14–1704
Nebraska	Computer Crime	Neb. Rev. Stat. §§ 28–1341 to 28–1348
	Identity Theft	Neb. Rev. Stat. §§ 28–636 to 28–640
	Data Breaches	Neb. Rev. Stat. §§ 87–801 to 87–808
Nevada	Computer Crime	Nev. Rev. Stat. §§ 205.473 to 205.513
	Identity Theft	Nev. Rev. Stat. §§ 205.461 to 205.4657

Nevada	False Personation	Nev. Rev. Stat. § 205.450
	Identity Theft Tools	Nev. Rev. Stat. § 205.605
	Data Breaches	Nev. Rev. Stat. §§ 603A.010 to 603A.290
New Hampshire	Computer Crime	N.H. Rev. Stat. §§ 638:16 to 638:19
	Spyware	N.H. Rev. Stat. §§ 359–H:1 to 359–H:6
	Identity Theft	N.H. Rev. Stat. §§ 638:25 to 638.27
	Identity Theft Tools	N.H. Rev. Stat. § 638.29
	Data Breaches	N.H. Rev. Stat. §§ 359–C:19 to 359–C:21
	Medical Information	N.H. Rev. Stat. § 332–I:5
New Jersey	Computer Crime	N.J. Rev. Stat. §§ 2C:20–23 to 34
	Identity Theft	N.J. Rev. Stat. §§ 2C:21–17 to 2C:21–17.6
	Data Breaches	N.J. Rev. Stat. §§ 56:8–161 to 56:8–166

New Mexico	Computer Crime	N.M. Stat. §§ 30–45–1 to 30–45–7
	Identity Theft	N.M. Stat. § 30–16–24.1
	Data Breaches	N.M. Stat. §§ 57–12C–1 to 57–12C–12
New York	Computer Crime	N.Y. Penal Law §§ 156.00 to 156.50
	Phishing	N.Y. Gen. Bus. § 390–b
	Identity Theft	N.Y. Penal Law §§ 190.77 to 190.84
	Identity Theft Tools	N.Y. Penal Law § 190.86
	False Personation	N.Y. Penal Law §§ 190.23 to 190.26
	Data Breaches	N.Y. Gen. Bus. § 899–aa
	Data Breaches at Government Agencies	McKinney's State Technology Law § 208
North Carolina	Computer Crime	N.C. Gen. Stat. §§ 14–453 to 14–458
	Identity Theft	N.C. Gen. Stat. § 14–113.20

North Carolina	Trafficking Stolen Identities	N.C. Gen. Stat. § 14–113.20A
	Data Breaches	N.C. Gen. Stat. § 75–65
	Records Disposal	N.C. Gen. Stat. § 75–64
North Dakota	Computer Crime	N.D. Cent. Code § 12.1–06.1–08
	Identity Theft	N.D. Cent. Code § 12.1–23–11
	Identity Theft Tools	N.D. Cent. Code § 12.1–23–17
	Data Breaches	N.D. Cent. Code §§ 51–30–01 to 51–30–07
Ohio	Computer Crime	Ohio Rev. Code § 2909.07(A)(6)
	Computer Crime	Ohio Rev. Code § 2913.04
	Telecommunications Fraud	Ohio Rev. Code § 2913.05
	Service Disruption	Ohio Rev. Code § 2909.04
	Identity Theft	Ohio Rev. Code § 2913.49
	Identity Theft Passport	Ohio Rev. Code § 109.94
	Data Breaches	Ohio Rev. Code §§ 1349.19, 1349.191, 1349.192

Ohio	Data Breaches at Government Agencies	Ohio Rev. Code § 1347.12
Oklahoma	Computer Crime	Okla. Stat. tit. 21, §§ 1951 to 1959
	Phishing	Okla. Stat. tit. 21, §§ 776.9 to 776.12
	Identity Theft	Okla. Stat. tit. 21, §§ 1533.1 to 1533.3
	Online Impersonation	Okla. Stat. tit. 12, § 1450
	False Personation	Okla. Stat. tit. 21, §§ 1531 to 1533
	Identity Theft Passport	Okla. Stat. tit. 22, § 19b
	Data Breaches	Okla. Stat. tit. 24, §§ 161 to 166
Oregon	Computer Crime	Or. Rev. Stat. § 164.377
	Identity Theft	Or. Rev. Stat. §§ 165.800 to 165.815
	Data Breaches	Or. Rev. Stat. § 646A.604
	Data Protection	Or. Rev. Stat. § 646A.622

Pennsylvania	Computer Crime	18 Pa. Stat. §§ 7601 to 7661
	Stored Communications	18 Pa. Stat. §§ 5741 to 5749
	Spyware	73 Pa. Stat. § 2330.3
	Identity Theft	18 Pa. Stat. § 4120
	Data Breaches	73 Pa. Stat. §§ 2301 to 2329
Rhode Island	Computer Crime	R.I. Gen. Laws §§ 11–52–1 to 11–52–8
	Email-Related Fraud	R.I. Gen. Laws § 11–52.1
	Software Fraud	R.I. Gen. Laws § 11–52.2
	Identity Theft	R.I. Gen. Laws §§ 11–49.1–1 to 11–49.1–5
	False Personation	R.I. Gen. Laws § 11–41–4
	Data Breaches	R.I. Gen. Laws §§ 11–49.3–1 to 11–49.3–6
South Carolina	Computer Crime	S.C. Code Ann. §§ 16–16–10 to 16–16–40
	Identity Theft	S.C. Code Ann. §§ 16–13–500 to 16–13–530

South Carolina	Data Breaches	S.C. Code Ann. § 39–1–90
	Data Breaches at Government Agencies	S.C. Code Ann. § 1–11–490
South Dakota	Computer Crime	S.D. Cod. Laws §§ 43–43B–1 to 43–43B–8
	Identity Theft	S.D. Cod. Laws §§ 22–40–8 to 22–40–18
	False Personation	S.D. Cod. Laws § 22–40–1
	Data Breaches	S.D. Cod. Laws §§ 22–40–19 to 22–40–26
Tennessee	Computer Crime	Tenn. Code §§ 39–14–601 to 39–14–605
	Phishing	Tenn. Code § 47–18–5201
	Identity Theft	Tenn. Code § 39–14–150
	Criminal Impersonation	Tenn. Code § 39–16–301
	Data Breaches	Tenn. Code §§ 47–18–2105 to 2107
Texas	Computer Crime	Tex. Penal Code § 33.02

Texas	Spyware	Tex. Bus. & Com. Code §§ 324.001 to 324.102
	Email-Related Fraud	Tex. Bus. & Com. Code §§ 325.001 to 325.006
	Identity Theft	Tex. Penal Code Ann. § 32.51
	Financial Information Theft	Tex. Penal Code Ann. § 31.17
	Data Breaches	Tex. Bus. & Com. Code § 521.053
	Data Breaches at Government Agencies	V.T.C.A., Government Code § 2054.1125
	Data Protection	Tex. Bus. & Com. Code § 521.052
Utah	Computer Crime	Utah Code §§ 76–6–702 to 76–6–705
	Phishing and Pharming	Utah Code §§ 13–40–201 to 13–40–204
	Spyware	Utah Code §§ 13–40–301 to 13–40–302
	Identity Theft	Utah Code §§ 76–6–1101 to 76–6–1105
	Data Breaches	Utah Code §§ 13–44–101 to 13–44–301

Vermont	Computer Crime	Vt. Stat. Ann. tit. 13, §§ 4101 to 4107
	Identity Theft	Vt. Stat. Ann. tit. 13, § 2030
	False Personation	Vt. Stat. Ann. tit. 13, § 2001
	Data Breaches	Vt. Stat. Ann. tit. 9, §§ 2430 to 2447
Virginia	Computer Crime	Va. Code §§ 18.2–152.1 to –152.15
	Identity Theft	Va. Code §§ 18.2–186.3 to 18.2–186.5
	Obtaining Personal Information by Trickery	Va. Code § 18.2–152.5:1
	Data Breaches	Va. Code § 18.2–186.6
	Medical Information	Va. Code § 32.1–127.1:05
	Tax Information	Va. Code § 58.1–341.2
Washington	Computer Crime	Wash. Rev. Code §§ 9A.90.010 to 9A.90.110
	Spyware	Wash. Rev. Code §§ 19.270.010 to 19.270.080
	Identity Theft	Wash. Rev. Code § 9.35.020

Washington	Financial Information Theft	Wash. Rev. Code § 9.35.010
	Data Breaches	Wash. Rev. Code §§ 19.255.010 and 19.255.020
West Virginia	Computer Crime	W. Va. Code §§ 61–3C–3 to 61–3C–21
	Identity Theft	W. Va. Code § 61–3–54
	Fraudulent Credit Cards	W. Va. Code § 61–3–24.a
	Data Breaches	W. Va. Code §§ 46A–2A–101 to 46A–2A–105
Wisconsin	Computer Crime	Wis. Stat. § 943.70
	Identity Theft	Wis. Stat. § 943.201
	Banned Devices	Wis. Stat. § 943.202
	Data Breaches	Wis. Stat. § 134.98
Wyoming	Computer Crime	Wyo. Stat. §§ 6–3–501 to 6–3–507
	Computer Trespass	Wyo. Stat. § 40–25–101
	Identity Theft	Wyo. Stat. § 6–3–901

| Wyoming | Online Impersonation | Wyo. Stat. § 6–3–902 |
| | Data Breaches | Wyo. Stat. § 40–12–502 |

INDEX

References are to Pages

FOURTH AMENDMENT
Cell site location data, 210, 211
GPS devices, 209, 211, 212
Location privacy, 211, 212
Private search doctrine, 208
Protection of cell phones, 210, 211, 212
Protection of digital evidence, 208, 209
Protection of metadata, 210
Reasonable expectation of privacy, 207, 211
Search incident to arrest, 210
Third party doctrine, 207, 208, 211
Wiretaps, 212

GENERAL DATA PROTECTION REGULATION, 242, 243,
    244, 245, 246, 247, 248
Application, 244
Consent, 245, 246
Controllers, 243, 244
Personal data, 243
Processing, 243, 244, 245, 246
Processors, 243
Rights of data subjects, 245, 246
Transmitting personal data, 246, 247

**GENETIC INFORMATION AND NONDISCRIMINATION
    ACT,** 234

GRAMM-LEACH-BLILEY ACT, 235

HACKBACK, See SELF-DEFENSE ONLINE

HACKER "HATS," 18, 155

HACKING, 17, 18

HACKING COMPETITIONS, 36

HACKING TEAM BREACH, 175

HACKTIVISM, 3, 4
Anonymous, 4

HEALTHCARE INFORMATION, 227, 232
Fair Credit Reporting Act, 232